Kevin Dundon's

BACK TO BASICS

Your Essential Step-by-step Cookbook

Kevin Dundon's

BACK TO BASICS

Your Essential Step-by-step Cookbook

MITCHELL BEAZLEY

For Catherine, Emily, Sophie & Tom

An Hachette UK Company
www.hachette.co.uk

First published in Great Britain in 2014 by
Mitchell Beazley, a division of
Octopus Publishing Group Ltd
Endeavour House
189 Shaftesbury Avenue,
London
WC2H 8JY
www.octopusbooks.co.uk
www.octopusbooksusa.com

Distributed in the US by
Hachette Book Group
1290 Avenue of the Americas
4th and 5th Floors
New York NY 10020 USA

Distributed in Canada by
Canadian Manda Group
664 Annette Street
Toronto, Ontario, Canada M6S 2C8

UK ISBN 978-1-84533-983-8
US ISBN 978-1-84533-985-2

A CIP catalogue record for this book is available
from the British Library

Printed and bound in Spain

10 9 8 7 6 5 4 3 2 1

Contents

Introduction

When I started to compile the recipes for this book, I really wanted to share with you how easy and straightforward cooking can be without using the abundance of convenience foods that have become commonplace in our lives. I would like this to be a cookbook that becomes well-thumbed and dog-eared through use, a book that the entire family will use, and I hope that my step-by-step methods will help your children master the fundamentals, making cooking an enjoyable and more understandable process.

Each chapter covers a basic ingredient, type of food or fundamental technique. Through the recipes you will learn key ways of cooking with a particular ingredient, from poaching eggs to mastering a soufflé, for example. In some cases I provide a basic technique – how to make a type of pastry, for instance – followed by a recipe that uses it. So, if you work your way through this book you'll acquire a great set of kitchen skills that will enable you to deal with just about anything and you can apply what you've learned to a host of other recipes. This book also works well as a kitchen 'bible' – you'll find something here for almost every occasion, whether that's a quick kitchen supper or a big Sunday lunch for friends and family.

I know from my own training and experience, and from teaching in my cookery school, just where the pitfalls lie, so I've included plenty of hints, tips and tricks of the trade, whether you need to know how to get your egg whites to form perfect peaks or the secret to crispy battered fish.

This book is a masterclass in the basics of good cooking, I hope you enjoy it.

Kevin

Eggs

Cooking Eggs

Ever wondered what's in an egg? Here's a brief synopsis.

Outside is the shell, the egg's first line of defence against bacteria. Inside is the gelatinous white – albumen – which represents about two-thirds of the egg's total weight and is high in protein and minerals. A clear membrane surrounds the yolk, and the fresher the egg, the stronger the membrane. The yolk itself is the egg's major source of vitamins and minerals, and is about one-third of the egg's total weight. The colour of the yolk, be it pale or deep yellow, does not affect the nutritional value. An average egg contains about 6g of protein and 70 calories.

To find out how fresh your eggs are, submerge them in cold water. The freshest will remain at the bottom of the bowl, while older eggs will float.

a

b

c

How to separate an egg cleanly

1   Set out two bowls and a ramekin. Take an egg and tap it sharply once against a work surface or chopping (cutting) board. **(a)** Hold it over the ramekin and use your thumbs to separate the shell along the crack.

2   Transfer the yolk from shell to shell, allowing the white to drop into the ramekin below. **(b)**

3   Place the yolk in one of the bowls, then tip the white into the other bowl. **(c)** If you see any tiny pieces of shell in the white, use a larger piece of shell to scoop it out. The sharp edge of the shell acts like a knife, breaking through the albumen to get the shell out cleanly.

Egg sizes

A-grade eggs come in four sizes:

Extra large	73g (2½oz) or more (US jumbo)
Large	63–73g (2¼–2½oz) (US extra large)
Medium	53–63g (1¾–2¼oz) (US large)
Small	below 53g (1¾oz) (US medium)

Two-cheese Omelette

Serves 1

2–3 large (US extra large) eggs
  (2 make a good breakfast,
  3 make a good lunch)
2 tbsp sunflower oil
50g (4 tbsp) clarified butter (see
  tip, page 16), or ordinary butter
50g (2oz) goats' cheese, crumbled
50g (½ cup) mature Cheddar cheese,
  grated
1 tbsp chopped chives

For the salad

1 red onion, thinly sliced
12 plum cherry tomatoes, halved
50g (½ cup) black olives, pitted
  and halved
100g (4 cups) rocket (arugula) leaves
2–3 tbsp Vinaigrette (see page 68)
Salt and black pepper

Served with a delicious side salad, this really is the perfect lunch. The omelette cooks very quickly, so make sure to have all the ingredients close to hand.

1   First prepare the salad. Place the onion, tomatoes, olives and rocket leaves in a bowl, then combine gently using your hands. Drizzle with some vinaigrette and season with salt and pepper. Set aside until required.

2   Crack the eggs into a bowl. Whisk until light and frothy.

3   Put the oil and butter into a 15cm (6 inch) nonstick frying pan over a medium heat. When the butter is frothy, pour in the eggs and move the back of a fork through them in small circles, allowing the uncooked egg to flow into the gaps. **(a)** Stop stirring once the eggs have begun to set but are still very moist in appearance.

4   Season with salt and pepper, then sprinkle with the cheeses and chives. Remove from the heat and use a palette knife or spatula to fold the omelette in half. **(b)** Leave to settle for a minute or two, then transfer to a serving plate and serve immediately with the salad.

a

b

Tips and ideas

- You can flavour omelettes with anything you like, such as chopped bacon, onion or mushrooms.

- The basic omelette can be used to make a frittata, which is a great way of using up leftover meat and vegetables. Just add them to the eggs, pour the mixture into the pan and cook for 2 minutes, then transfer to the oven (preheated to 180°C/350°F/gas mark 4) for 15 minutes.

Basil Scrambled Eggs with Goats' Cheese

Serves 2

6 eggs
25g (2 tbsp) cold butter, cubed
1 tbsp cream or crème fraîche
100g (4oz) soft goats' cheese,
  preferably Boilíe
75g (2 cups) basil leaves, plus a few
  extra to garnish
Salt and black pepper
2 slices of soda bread, toasted
6–9 semi-dried cherry tomatoes
  (optional)

Scrambled eggs are a treat that never fails on a Sunday morning. Served here with goats' cheese and basil, they are bursting with flavour.

1   Break the eggs into a bowl and whisk until light and frothy. **(a)**

2   Pour the eggs into a nonstick frying pan, add the butter and cook over a medium-low heat, gently pushing them with a wooden spoon from one side to the other in four different directions, making sure to go right to the bottom of the pan. **(b)** Do this for 3–5 minutes, until the eggs start to clump but are still soft and creamy.

3   Remove from the heat and stir in the crème fraîche, goats' cheese and basil leaves. Season with salt and pepper.

4   Serve on the toast, placing the tomatoes (if using) and a few extra basil leaves on top.

a

b

Tips and ideas

- The trick to making creamy scrambled eggs is to take them off the heat while they still look wet, but not runny. They will continue to cook from the residual heat, but this can dry them out if they are cooked too long in the first instance.

- Always scramble eggs over a low heat. It might take longer for them to cook, but it will give you more control over the consistency and avoid the eggs becoming brown or overcooked.

Eggs Benedict

Serves 4

8 slices of streaky (fatty) bacon
  or cooked ham
4 slices of bread or English muffin
50g (4 tbsp) butter, at room
  temperature
4 eggs
1 tbsp vinegar
Pinch of salt
1 tbsp snipped chives

For the hollandaise sauce
2 egg yolks
2 tbsp white wine vinegar
1 tbsp lemon juice
White pepper, to taste
225g (2 sticks) clarified butter
  (see tip below)

Tips and ideas

- To clarify butter, place the required amount in a small saucepan and leave to melt over a very low heat. Leave to stand for a few minutes, then skim off any foam. **(a)** Spoon the remaining butter into a sealable plastic container, ensuring no sediment is present, and use as required. The eggs can be partly cooked in advance if you like. Poach them for 2 minutes, then transfer to a bowl of cold water until you are ready to serve them later on. To reheat, simply pop them into a saucepan of hot water for 1 minute.

- Try to use really fresh eggs so that the yolk stays well in the centre of the white.

- Using a deep saucepan allows the egg to start cooking before it hits the bottom of the pan and results in a better shape.

With only three principal components – bread, poached eggs and hollandaise – this is a simple dish, but it requires care and patience. The sauce in particular can curdle if you tackle it too fast, so keep calm, follow the steps and it will work out perfectly.

1 First make the hollandaise. Bring a saucepan of water to the boil, then keep it on a very gentle simmer.

2 Put the egg yolks into a large, spotlessly clean heatproof bowl and add the vinegar, lemon juice and pepper. **(b)** Set the bowl over the pan of simmering water, making sure the bottom of the bowl does not touch the water. Whisk until the mixture becomes light and creamy in both colour and consistency. **(c)** You need to be very careful because the line between creamy sauce and scrambled eggs is very fine indeed.

3 Slowly pour in the clarified butter a little at a time, whisking constantly to prevent curdling. **(d)** If you can't manage this easily using both hands, you can take the bowl off the saucepan while adding the butter, then return it to the pan while whisking it in. You may find this a bit tricky, but do persevere – the end result is worth the effort. If, after adding all the butter, the sauce is a little thick for your liking, whisk in a drop of cold water. Cover the bowl with clingfilm (plastic wrap) and set aside.

4 If using bacon, preheat the grill (broiler) on its highest setting. When hot, grill (broil) the bacon for 3–4 minutes on each side. Set aside and keep warm.

5 Place the bread on the grill (broiler) pan and toast both sides. Spread with the butter.

6 Next, poach the eggs. Crack 1 egg into a small bowl. Line a plate with kitchen paper (paper towels).

7 Fill a wide, deep saucepan with a 10cm (4 inch) depth of water. Add the vinegar and salt and bring to the boil over a medium-high heat. Reduce the heat so the water is just simmering, with small bubbles rising from the bottom and small ripples across the top.

8 Using a whisk or wooden spoon, stir the water in one direction to create a whirlpool, then slide the egg into the centre of it, as close to the water as possible. (The whirlpool will help to give your poached eggs a neat

a

b

c

d

shape.) **(e)** Cook without stirring for 2–3 minutes if you like a semi-soft yolk, or 3–4 minutes for a firm yolk. **(f)** Carefully skim off any foam that rises to the surface.

9   Using a slotted spoon, lift out the egg, place on the prepared plate and keep warm. **(g)** Cook the other eggs in the same way.

10 Place the toasted bread on serving plates, top with the bacon and eggs and spoon over the hollandaise sauce. Sprinkle with the chives and serve.

e

f

Eggs Benedict Variations

Irish-style Eggs Benedict – replace the bacon or ham with smoked salmon.

Eggs Florentine – replace the bacon or ham with 200g (1 cup) cooked spinach.

Hollandaise Sauce Variations

Learning how to make hollandaise is extremely useful because it can be used as the basis of several other sauces.

Sauce Bavaroise – add 50ml (¼ cup) cream, 1 tsp horseradish and 1 tsp thyme leaves.

Sauce Crème Fleurette – add 20ml (4 tsp) crème fraîche.

Sauce Dijon – add 20g (4 tsp) Dijon mustard.

Sauce Maltaise – replace the vinegar and lemon juice with the juice of 1 blood orange and the blanched zest of half.

Sauce Mousseline – fold in 100ml (½ cup) whipped cream.

Sauce Noisette – replace the clarified butter with 225ml (1 cup) browned butter (beurre noisette – see page 156).

g

Fresh Tagliatelle Carbonara

Serves 4

Olive oil, for frying
300g (11oz) streaky (fatty) bacon, diced
3 egg yolks
75g (1 cup) Parmesan cheese, freshly grated, plus extra to serve
Salt and cracked black pepper

For the pasta – makes 350g (12oz)
300g (2⅓ cups) Italian '00' flour, plus extra for dusting
2 eggs plus 3 egg yolks
1 tsp olive oil
1 tsp salt

Tips and ideas

- The fresh pasta dough can be flavoured with fresh herbs, pesto or spices if you like.

- The resting time for fresh pasta is very important because it allows the ingredients to settle and bind together.

- Spelt flour, which is low in gluten, can be used instead of Italian '00' flour if you like, but if you do so, I recommend making lasagne sheets rather than tagliatelle. You may need to purchase '00' flour online.

- If you want to reduce the egg content of the pasta, simply replace the eggs with the same weight of water.

- Using ready-made dried pasta will make a quicker version of the dish, but with a drier texture.

- You can also add 50ml (¼ cup) double (heavy) cream if you like.

- I recommend using a machine to roll out fresh pasta, as it is tricky to get the correct result by hand.

This is a very traditional carbonara recipe made with egg yolks for extra enrichment.

1 First make the pasta dough. Sift the flour into a bowl, then add the eggs and yolks, the olive oil and salt. Mix by hand or pulse in a food processor until a soft dough forms. **(a)** It should be elastic and not sticky. Place in a clean bowl, cover with clingfilm (plastic wrap) and leave to rest for 30 minutes. **(b)**

2 Cut the dough into 4 equal pieces and cover with a clean, damp tea (dish) towel.

3 Take one piece of dough and flatten into a rectangle using the palm of your hand. **(c)** Set the pasta machine (if using) to its widest setting and dust the rollers with flour. **(d)** Pass the dough through, then flour the rollers again and pass it through once more. **(e)** Repeat the flouring and rolling three or four more times until smooth. Reduce the roller width to the next setting and pass the dough through as before. Repeat the process, reducing the setting each time until the dough is paper thin. Alternatively, flour a work surface and use a rolling pin to roll out the dough as thinly as possible.

4 To cut the pasta into tagliatelle, loosely roll it up from the shortest side. Trim off and discard the ends. Using a sharp knife, cut through the roll at 5mm (¼ inch) intervals. **(f)** Unravel the pasta strips over the handle of a wooden spoon and leave to dry for 5-10 minutes. **(g/h)**

5 Meanwhile, heat a little olive oil in a large sauté pan and fry the bacon until crispy. Transfer to a plate lined with kitchen paper (paper towels).

6 Put the egg yolks and Parmesan into a bowl, season lightly with cracked black pepper and beat together.

7 Bring a large saucepan of water to the boil, add 1 teaspoon salt, then cook the tagliatelle for 2-3 minutes, until al dente. Stir once or twice during the cooking process to ensure that it does not stick together.

8 Drain the pasta and return it to the saucepan, off the heat. Add the bacon and the egg mixture and stir gently with a wooden spoon to ensure the pasta is fully coated.

9 Serve immediately in warmed bowls, and sprinkle with a little extra Parmesan and cracked black pepper if you like.

e

f

g

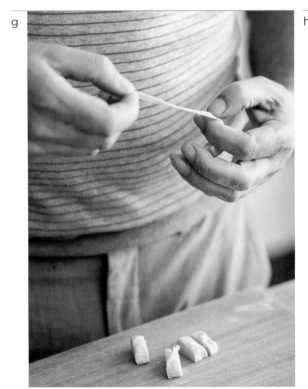

h

Mini Meringue Kisses

Makes 12–15

3 large (US extra large) egg whites,
about 100g (4oz) in total
200g (1 cup) caster (superfine) sugar
½ tsp cornflour (cornstarch)
½ tsp white wine vinegar
½ tsp vanilla extract
150ml (⅔ cup) double (heavy) cream,
whipped
12–15 strawberries or other summer
berries, halved if large
Icing (confectioners') sugar, for
dusting (optional)

When making the meringue mixture, it's important to add an acid element after the sugar has been incorporated. I use vinegar, but lemon juice could be used instead. It helps ensure a crisp outer crust and a soft, chewy centre.

1   Preheat the oven to 120°C/250°F/gas mark ½. Line a baking sheet with nonstick baking (parchment) paper.

2   Put the egg whites into a spotlessly clean bowl and whisk on full speed until they form stiff peaks. **(a)**

3   Reduce the speed of the mixer and add the sugar a little at a time, beating thoroughly. **(b)**

4   When all the sugar has been incorporated, add the cornflour and vinegar and whisk again on high speed until the mixture is glossy and stays put when the bowl is turned upside down.

5   Fold in the vanilla extract to flavour the meringue, then spoon the mixture into a piping (pastry) bag fitted with a 1cm (½ inch) star nozzle (tip).

6   Pipe 24–30 walnut-sized blobs of meringue on to the prepared baking sheet, making sure they do not touch one another.

7   Bake for 25–30 minutes, until firm to the touch but still soft in the middle. I normally leave mine to cool in the oven with the door ajar.

8   Carefully lift the meringues off the paper and sandwich them together with some whipped cream and berries. Serve within a few hours of making, dusted with icing sugar (if using).

Tips and ideas

•   It is important that your bowl is spotlessly clean or the egg whites will not form peaks. To be absolutely sure the bowl has no fat residue, you can rub a cut lemon around it.

•   To ensure the sugar is fully incorporated into the egg white, pinch the mixture between your index finger and thumb. If it feels grainy, keep beating and testing until it feels smooth.

a

b

Berries Sabayon

Serves 4

1 vanilla pod or bean
150ml (⅔ cup) sweet wine or fortified
  wine (e.g. Sauternes, port or even
  champagne)
75g (⅓ cup) caster (superfine) sugar
3 egg yolks
250g (1¼ cups) strawberries,
  quartered
200g (1½ cups) blueberries

A sabayon is a dessert made with egg yolks, sugar and wine beaten together over heat until thick and foamy. It is best served hot or warm.

1   Split the vanilla pod in half lengthways, then scrape the seeds into a large heatproof bowl with the back of knife. **(a)**

2   Add the wine, sugar and egg yolks, then whisk together.

3   Set the bowl over a saucepan of gently simmering water, making sure the bottom of the bowl does not touch the water. Whisk vigorously until the mixture becomes frothy and stiff. **(b)** You can remove the bowl from the pan for a brief time and slow down the speed of whisking if you need a short break. The sabayon is ready when the mixture is thick and holds its shape when dropped from the whisk back into the bowl.

4   Pile the berries into individual serving glasses and pour the warm sabayon over them. Serve immediately.

a

b

Tips and ideas

• Use a blowtorch to caramelize the top of the sabayon.

• For a non-alcoholic version of sabayon, replace the wine with lemonade (lemon-flavoured soda pop).

• Use whatever fresh fruit is in season. Peaches, apricots and pineapple all work well.

Raspberry Soufflés

Serves 4

20g (1½ tbsp) softened butter
175g (¾ cup plus 2 tbsp) caster
  (superfine) sugar, plus extra for
  dusting
200g (1⅔ cups) raspberries, at room
  temperature
Juice of ½ lemon
3 tbsp icing (confectioners') sugar
100g (½ cup) crème fraîche
3 egg yolks, at room temperature
4 egg whites, at room temperature
½ tsp xanthan gum (see tip below)

Tips and ideas

- Adding xanthan gum to the egg
  whites gives them greater stability
  and ensures a decent rise. This very
  useful ingredient is available in
  most supermarkets or online, but
  take care not to add too much or it
  will actually stop the soufflés rising.

- Replace the raspberries with other
  flavours, such as lemon juice, apple
  juice or chocolate sauce.

- Place a quenelle (rounded spoonful)
  of raspberry or vanilla ice cream on
  top of each soufflé if you like.

These little soufflés are an impressive dessert, but they will need to have all your attention until the last minute. Prepare and set out all the ingredients beforehand so you can work quickly.

1   Butter four 120ml (½ cup) ramekins or heatproof teacups using upward strokes. **(a)** Place in the refrigerator for 5 minutes, then brush with a second coating of butter. Sprinkle some caster sugar over the butter and shake out the excess. **(b)** Return to the refrigerator until required.

2   Put the raspberries and lemon juice into a blender or food processor and blend to a purée. Pass the mixture through a fine sieve or strainer to remove any seeds. **(c)** Measure out 50g (¼ cup) of the purée and place in a small bowl. Mix the remainder with 1 tablespoon of the icing sugar and set aside.

3   Preheat the oven to 180°C/350°F/gas mark 4.

4   Place the crème fraîche, egg yolks and measured amount of raspberry purée in a bowl and beat until combined. **(d)**

5   In a spotlessly clean bowl, whisk the egg whites until they form soft peaks. **(e)** Gradually beat in the caster sugar one-third at a time. Add the xanthan gum with the last third of the sugar and whisk again until stiffer.

6   Using a large plastic spatula or metal spoon, fold one-quarter of the egg whites into the crème fraîche mixture. Once combined, fold in the remaining egg whites, stirring from the side through the centre. **(f)** Do not overmix as you want to keep in the air bubbles.

7   Spoon the soufflé mixture into the prepared dishes, then run your thumb around the rims to remove any splashes. **(g/h)**

8   Place the dishes on a baking sheet and bake for 10–12 minutes, until the soufflés are risen and golden.

9   Quickly dust with the remaining icing sugar and serve the remaining raspsberry purée in a jug (pitcher). The soufflés should hold for 2–3 minutes before collapsing.

Pastry

Shortcrust Pastry

Makes 450g (1lb) dough

300g (2⅓ cups) plain (all-purpose)
  flour
Pinch of salt
150g (1¼ sticks) cold butter,
  finely cubed
2–3 tbsp ice-cold water

The pastry known as shortcrust is the type most often used in baking, and can be either sweet or savoury. Like most pastries, its basic ingredients are flour, fat and water, but it is essential to measure them accurately and to avoid overhandling them. Always try to use the best ingredients to get the best results. The dough will keep for 3 days in the refrigerator, or up to 2 months in the freezer.

1   Sift the flour into a large bowl and add the salt and butter. **(a)** Using your fingers, rub the mixture together until it resembles very fine breadcrumbs. **(b)**

2   Mix in just enough of the water to form a dough, then knead gently to bind it together. **(c/d)** Shape into a thick rectangle, wrap in clingfilm (plastic wrap) and leave to rest in the refrigerator for 10 minutes.

3   Use as required, kneading it for a minute or so before rolling out.

Tips and ideas

- To enrich the dough add 1 egg instead of the water.

- Try to work the dough as quickly as possible. The more it is kneaded, the more elastic it becomes, which causes it to shrink while baking.

- Overhandling pastry also causes the gluten strands to toughen, so work quickly with cold kitchen utensils.

- I sometimes like to roll the dough straight away and let it rest at that point before using.

- If freezing the dough, freeze it already rolled, between two sheets of nonstick baking (parchment) paper, and wrapped in clingfilm (plastic wrap). Use within 2 months.

Shortcrust Variations

Herb Pastry – add 2 tbsp dried herbs, such as thyme, oregano or a mixture, to the dry ingredients in the basic pastry.

Parmesan Pastry – add 20g (4 tsp) grated Parmesan cheese to the dry ingredients in the basic pastry.

Pesto Pastry – add 2 tbsp basil pesto to the dry ingredients in the basic pastry.

a

b

c

d

Winter Root Vegetable Tart

Serves 8

2 tbsp olive oil
Plain (all-purpose) flour, for dusting
¾ quantity Shortcrust Pastry
  (see page 34)
300g (11oz) kale
1 carrot, very finely diced
1 parsnip, very finely diced
Salt and black pepper
1 egg plus 2 egg yolks
200ml (¾ cup plus 2 tbsp) double
  (heavy) cream
1 tbsp chopped chives

Best served warm with a lightly dressed salad, this tart is full of flavour, and can be made with whatever vegetables you have to hand.

1 Preheat the oven to 180°C/350°F/gas mark 4. Use half the oil to grease a 24cm (9½ inch) tart tin, then dust it with flour.

2 Lightly flour a work surface and roll out the dough to a thickness of 3mm (⅛ inch). Use to line the prepared tin, then leave to rest in the refrigerator for 15–20 minutes.

3 Prick the base of the pastry case (shell) with a fork, then line with a triple layer of clingfilm (plastic wrap). **(a)** Fill with baking beans (pie weights) or rice, cover with another layer of clingfilm and bake for 20 minutes. **(b)** Remove the clingfilm and weights, reduce the heat to 160°C/325°F/gas mark 3 and bake the pastry for a further 10 minutes.

4 Meanwhile, cook the kale in a saucepan of boiling salted water for 2 minutes, or until just tender. Drain, then refresh immediately in a bowl of iced water. Drain and set aside.

5 Place the remaining oil in a saucepan over a medium heat. When hot, add the carrot and parsnip and cook for 3–4 minutes, until softened and lightly coloured. Add the kale, season with salt and pepper and toss together. Remove from the heat.

6 Put the egg, egg yolks and cream into a bowl, season with salt and pepper and whisk until combined. Stir in the chives.

7 Arrange the vegetables in the pastry case, then pour three-quarters of the egg mixture over them. Carefully add the remaining egg mixture, making sure it doesn't overflow, and bake the tart for 30 minutes, or until the egg is set with just a slight wobble. Leave to stand for 5 minutes.

8 Run a palette knife (spatula) around the tart to loosen it, then lift it on to a serving platter and serve warm.

a

b

Sweet Pastry

Makes 450g (1lb) dough

250g (2¼ sticks) butter, at room
   temperature
150g (1¼ cups) icing (confectioners')
   sugar
2 eggs, beaten
500g (4 cups) plain (all-purpose) flour

The method used here is a little
unconventional, but we've been using
it in our kitchen for the last few years
and it produces great results. The dough
will keep for 3 days in the refrigerator, or
up to a month in the freezer.

1 Put the butter and sugar into a bowl and beat until light
   and fluffy, then beat in the eggs with a wooden spoon.
   (a) The mixture will look a little split, but don't panic. **(b)**

2 Sift the flour into a large bowl and make a well in the
   centre. Pour the egg mixture into the well and gradually
   mix together to form a smooth dough. **(c/d)** Shape into
   a rectangle, wrap in clingfilm (plastic wrap) and leave
   to rest in the refrigerator for at least 30 minutes.

3 Use as required, kneading it for a minute or so before
   rolling out.

Tips and ideas

- Unlike savoury shortcrust dough,
  which can be rolled out straight
  away if you like, sweet pastry uses
  creamed butter and therefore needs
  to be chilled before rolling or it will
  stick to the work surface.

- Use a generous dusting of flour
  when rolling out this dough to
  ensure it doesn't stick, and check
  it between each roll.

- To roll dough into a neat, regular
  circle, move it by 3mm (⅛ inch)
  between each roll.

- Sweet pastry dough is more fragile
  than savoury, and will feel lighter
  in the mouth.

Sweet Pastry Variations

Almond Pastry – replace 50g (⅓ cup) of the flour with the
same amount of ground almonds.

Chocolate Pastry – replace 50g (⅓ cup) of the flour with
the same amount of unsweetened cocoa powder.

Autumn Tartlets with Cinnamon Cream

Makes 6

Butter, for greasing
Plain (all-purpose) flour, for dusting
½ quantity Sweet Pastry
  (see page 38)
2 fresh figs, finely sliced
400g (3½ cups) mixed berries
  (e.g. redcurrants, raspberries,
  blackberries, blueberries)
Juice of 2 lemons
40g (¼ cup) brown sugar

For the cinnamon cream
300ml (1¼ cups) double (heavy)
  cream
2½ tbsp icing (confectioners') sugar
2 tsp ground cinnamon

I like to make these tartlets during summertime, as well as in the autumn. They're perfect with soft fruits, such as strawberries, raspberries and blueberries. I also recommend using fresh apricots drizzled with honey – simply delicious!

1   Preheat the oven to 180°C/350°F/gas mark 4. Grease six 10cm (4 inch) loose-bottomed tart tins, then dust them with flour.

2   Generously flour a work surface and roll out the dough to a thickness of 3mm (⅛ inch). Use to line the prepared tins, then leave to rest in the refrigerator for 20–30 minutes.

3   Prick the bases of the pastry cases (shells) with a fork, then line with greaseproof (wax) paper or clingfilm (plastic wrap) and fill with baking beans (pie weights) or rice. Bake for 15 minutes, then remove the lining and weights, reduce the heat to 160°C/325°F/gas mark 3 and bake the pastry for a further 10 minutes. Carefully remove the pastry cases from their tins and place on a wire rack to cool.

4   Place the figs and 250g (2¼ cups) of the berries in a bowl. Sprinkle half the lemon juice over them, cover with clingfilm and set aside.

5   Put the brown sugar and remaining lemon juice in a small saucepan over a medium heat. Leave to dissolve, without stirring, until a golden blond caramel forms.

6   Add the remaining berries and stir gently for 2–3 minutes. Pass the mixture through a sieve or strainer and leave to cool for 5 minutes.

7   Meanwhile, put the cream, icing sugar and cinnamon into a large bowl and whisk until soft peaks form.

8   Fold the cooled caramel mixture into the reserved berries and figs.

9   To serve, spoon some cinnamon cream into each pastry case and top with the berry mixture.

Tips and ideas

- For a firmer mixture, replace the whipped cream with strawberry mousse, *crème patissière* (see page 52) or chocolate ganache, or lemon curd lightened with whipped cream.

Suet Pastry

Makes 350g (12oz) dough

225g (1¾ cups) plain (all-purpose)
  flour, plus extra for dusting
1 tsp salt
2 tsp baking powder
100g (½ cup) shredded suet, or
  equal parts of butter and lard,
  finely chopped
2–3 tbsp cold water

Used in steamed puddings or baked in pies,
suet pastry is sharper in flavour than other
pastries, and is wonderfully light and airy.

1   Sift the flour into a large bowl with the salt and baking
    powder. Add the suet and mix together well. **(a)**

2   Mix in just enough of the water to form a dough. **(b)** For
    safety's sake, add the water a little at a time.

3   Transfer the dough to a well-floured work surface and
    knead for a few moments. **(c/d)** Shape into a rectangle,
    wrap in clingfilm (plastic wrap) and leave to rest in the
    refrigerator for 20 minutes.

4   Use as required.

Suet Pastry Variation

Duck Fat 'Suet' Pastry – put 1 egg and 65g (⅓ cup) duck fat
into a bowl and beat until smooth. Mix in 50g (¼ cup) caster
(superfine) sugar and 1 scant tsp salt. Fold in 200g (1⅔ cups)
plain (all-purpose) flour and 1 tsp baking powder. When
a dough forms, knead until smooth, then use in the same
way as suet pastry.

Traditional Steak and Kidney Pudding

Serves 4-6

250g (9oz) lambs' kidneys
50g (4 tbsp) butter
1 tbsp rapeseed (canola) oil
2 onions, diced
3 garlic cloves
625g (1¼lb) beef stewing steak
  (boneless beef chuck or round),
  cut into large cubes
200g (3 cups) button mushrooms,
  quartered
Salt and black pepper
2 tbsp plain (all-purpose) flour, plus
  extra for dusting
Pinch of cayenne pepper or smoked
  paprika
750ml (3 cups) hot Beef Stock
  (see page 86)
100ml (½ cup) red wine
1 tbsp tomato purée (paste)
1 bay leaf
3-4 sprigs of thyme
1 tbsp Worcestershire sauce
1 quantity Suet Pastry (see page 42)
Butter, for greasing
1 egg yolk mixed with 1 tbsp milk,
  for brushing

Steak and kidney pudding is one of those comforting dishes that will always leave the family satisfied.

1   Wash the kidneys and cut them in half. Remove the tubes and peel off the outer membrane.

2   Put the butter and oil into a large saucepan over a medium heat, add the onions and garlic and cook for 3-4 minutes, until softened.

3   Add the beef and kidneys to the pan and cook for 3-5 minutes, until the meat is brown and sealed all over.

4   Add the mushrooms, season with salt and pepper and fry for a further 2 minutes, shaking the pan to combine.

5   Mix the flour and cayenne pepper in a small bowl, then sprinkle over the beef mixture. Stir well to coat, then cook for 1-2 minutes, until the flour has coloured too (this will give an extra flavour and thickness to the sauce later on).

6   Gradually pour in the stock and stir constantly until the sauce begins to thicken.

7   Add the wine, tomato purée, bay leaf, thyme sprigs and Worcestershire sauce. Stir and bring to the boil, then cover and simmer for 1½-2 hours, until the beef is tender. Remove from the heat and leave to cool.

8   Preheat the oven to 160°C/325°F/gas mark 3.

9   Set aside one-quarter of the dough, then roll out the remainder on a lightly floured surface. Grease a 1 litre (1 quart) deep ovenproof dish and line with the dough, making sure any splits are well sealed. Spoon the meat into the dish, reserving the gravy to thicken and serve separately. Roll out the reserved dough to fit the top. Dampen the pastry around the edge of the dish with egg wash and place the lid on top. Trim off the excess with a knife, then flute the edges by pressing the back of a knife into the pastry at regular intervals. **(a)** Lightly prick the surface with a fork and brush all over with more egg wash.

10 Place in a roasting pan in the oven and pour in enough boiling water to come halfway up the outside of the dish. Steam for 2-2½ hours. Keep an eye on the steamer and, when necessary, top it up with boiling water to maintain a consistent level around the dish. Do not use cold water, as it will make the pudding heavy.

a

Puff Pastry

Makes 1.2kg (2½lb) dough

500g (4 cups) plain (all-purpose) flour,
  plus extra for dusting
2 tsp salt
550g (5 sticks) cold butter, cubed
2 tbsp white wine vinegar
200ml (¾ cup plus 2 tbsp) cold water

Tips and ideas

- As you fold, mark the dough with your fingerprint to remind you how many folds you have done.

- It is important to keep the dough cold for rolling between turns; if the butter is soft, return the dough to the refrigerator for 10–20 minutes.

- Dust off any excess flour left on the dough or it won't rise properly when baked.

- To flavour the pastry you can omit the vinegar and add the same amount of very clear, cold chicken, beef or fish stock, or squid ink.

Puff pastry is a challenge, but not as difficult as generally assumed. The folding and rolling, which create multiple layers that expand as the pastry bakes, take time and patience, but the result is really satisfying. If you're pushed for time, good-quality frozen pastry is readily available from supermarkets.

1 Place the flour, salt and 200g (1¾ sticks) of the butter in a large bowl. Using your fingers, rub the mixture together until it resembles breadcrumbs. Make a well in the centre and pour in the vinegar and water. Use your fingertips to form a dough. Shape into a ball, wrap in clingfilm (plastic wrap) and leave to rest in the refrigerator for 1 hour.

2 Place the chilled dough on a lightly floured work surface and use a sharp knife make a cross in the top, cutting about halfway through. **(a)** Roll out the quarters from the centre so they look like four large flaps. **(b)**

3 Dot the remaining butter cubes all over the dough. **(c)** Fold the pastry flaps over them, brushing off the excess flour as you do so. **(d)** Roll the dough into a rectangle approximately 60 x 30cm (24 x 12 inches), then fold the pastry in three by bringing the right side into the centre and overlapping it with the left side. **(e)** Rotate and repeat the rolling and folding once more. **(f)** Wrap in clingfilm and chill for 20 minutes. Repeat the rolling and folding five more times, wrapping the pastry in clingfilm and chilling for 20 minutes after every second turn. The pastry is ready to be used after the final turn. (The pastry will have been rolled and folded seven times in total.)

4 Use as required. The dough will keep for a week in the refrigerator, and 2 months in the freezer.

Salmon en Croûte

Serves 4

25g (2 tbsp) butter
225g (3 cups) mushrooms, thinly
  sliced
400g (13 cups) spinach
¾ quantity Puff Pastry (see page 46)
Plain (all-purpose) flour, for dusting
1 egg, beaten
750g (1½lb) side of salmon, skin
  removed
Salt and black pepper
2 eggs, hard-boiled, peeled and sliced
2 shallots, thinly sliced
1 tbsp chopped dill
1 tsp chopped lemon thyme
1 quantity Hollandaise Sauce, to serve
  (see page 16)

Also known as a *coulibiac*, this is a French adaptation of a Russian fish pie made in loaf form. Smoked cod or haddock can be used instead of salmon. For a vegetarian alternative, use seasonal vegetables – perhaps wilted greens, asparagus, peas and artichoke hearts in springtime, and kale, leeks or wild mushrooms during the winter.

1   Melt the butter in a large frying pan over a high heat. Add the mushrooms and sauté for 2 minutes, or until cooked through. Stir in the spinach, than remove from the heat and leave to wilt.

2   Cut the pastry in half and place on a lightly floured work surface. Roll each piece into a sheet about 30 x 20cm (12 x 8 inches), then brush the surface of the sheets with the beaten egg.

3   Place the spinach mixture on 1 sheet of pastry, leaving a 2.5cm (1 inch) gap all around the edge.

4   Lay the salmon on the spinach and season with salt and pepper. **(a)**

5   Put the sliced eggs, shallots and herbs in a bowl, mix together, then arrange on top of the salmon.

6   Place the remaining sheet of pastry over the filling and use a fork to press lightly all around the edge to seal. **(b)** Brush the pastry with beaten egg and leave to rest in the refrigerator for 10 minutes.

7   Preheat the oven to 180°C/350°F/gas mark 4.

8   With the tip of a sharp knife, make very light incisions in the pastry, curving them to look like fish scales. You can also mark out the eyes and gills if you like.

9   Transfer the salmon to a baking sheet and bake for 30–35 minutes, until puffed and golden brown. Leave to stand for 15 minutes.

10 Place the salmon on a serving platter, and serve the Hollandaise Sauce separately.

a

b

Choux Pastry

Makes about 325g (11½oz) dough

50g (4 tbsp) butter, cubed
1 tsp caster (superfine) sugar
50ml (¼ cup) milk
85ml (⅓ cup) water
75g (⅔ cup) plain (all-purpose) flour
2 large (US extra large) eggs

Choux differs from other pastries in that it is cooked in a pan before being baked. Like many good things, it takes a little time to make, but the resulting smooth and shiny dough can be used to create fantastic pastries, such as profiteroles, éclairs and cream puffs.

1   Place the butter, sugar, milk and water in a saucepan and bring to the boil. **(a)** Remove from the heat and immediately stir in the flour. **(b)** Place over a medium heat and stir briskly until the mixture forms a soft dough and leaves the side of the saucepan dry. **(c)** Transfer to a bowl.

2   Without cooling the mixture, add the eggs one at a time, beating thoroughly after each addition. The dough should be smooth and glossy. **(d)**

3   Use straight away as required.

Tips and ideas

• Don't over-boil the liquid and butter mixture; bring it to the boil but don't allow it to evaporate.

• When cooking choux pastry, add a few splashes of water to the baking sheet before putting it in the oven. This will create steam and help the choux to rise.

Chocolate Éclairs

Makes 12

1 quantity Choux Pastry (see page 50)
1 egg yolk mixed with 1 tsp milk,
  for brushing

For the crème patissière
4 egg yolks
100g (½ cup) caster (superfine) sugar
25g (3 tbsp) plain (all-purpose) flour
350ml (1½ cups) milk
Seeds from ½ vanilla pod or bean or
  1 tsp vanilla extract

For the icing
100g (¾ cup) icing (confectioners')
  sugar
Juice of ½ lemon
1 tsp unsweetened cocoa powder

Tips and ideas

• Pastry cream can be flavoured in
  many different ways. Try adding a
  little rum, brandy, whisky, Tia Maria,
  Irish cream liqueur, Cointreau, fruit
  purée or melted chocolate.

• The icing can also be flavoured
  differently. For coffee éclairs, for
  example, replace the cocoa powder
  with ½ tsp instant coffee dissolved
  in 1 tsp boiling water.

• Colouring or coloured ingredients
  can also be added to adapt the éclairs
  to the occasion. On St Patrick's Day,
  for example, add pistachio paste to
  the *crème patissière*, and green food
  colouring to the icing.

Traditionally, chocolate éclairs are filled
with custard-like *crème patissière* and
are partially covered in chocolate icing.

1   Preheat the oven to 160°C/325°F/gas mark 3. Line a
    baking sheet with nonstick baking (parchment) paper.

2   Spoon the dough into a piping (pastry) bag fitted with
    a plain 1cm (½ inch) nozzle (tip). Pipe 6cm (2½ inch)
    strips on to the prepared baking sheet, spacing them
    at least 2.5cm (1 inch) apart. **(a)**

3   Dip a fork into a bowl of hot water and smooth the top
    of each choux strip. **(b)**

4   Brush the top of each strip with a very light coating
    of egg wash. **(c)**

5   Bake for 20–25 minutes, until golden brown outside
    and dry inside. Transfer to a wire rack to cool. **(d)**

6   Meanwhile, prepare the *crème patissière*. Put the egg
    yolks and sugar in a bowl and whisk until light and
    creamy. Beat in the flour, then set aside.

7   Place the milk and vanilla seeds in a saucepan and bring
    slowly to the boil. Remove immediately from the heat
    and pour half into the egg mixture, whisking constantly
    as you do so.

8   Add the egg mixture to the milk remaining in the pan
    and whisk constantly over a low-medium heat until
    simmering. Continue to cook and whisk for 2 minutes,
    or until the mixture has thickened and lifts off the
    bottom of the pan.

9   Transfer the *crème patissière* to a clean container and
    place a sheet of clingfilm (plastic wrap) directly on top
    to prevent a skin forming. **(e)** Leave to cool for 2–3 hours,
    until set.

10 When you're ready to assemble the éclairs, use a small
    sharp knife to cut the buns in half horizontally. **(f)** Pipe
    or spoon the *crème patissière* into the bottom half of
    each one. **(g)**

11 Put all the icing ingredients into a bowl and mix until
    smooth. Dip the upper surface of the remaining pastry
    halves into the icing and place them on the filled lower
    halves. **(h)** The éclairs are best enjoyed on the day they
    are made.

a

b

c

d

e

f

g

h

Savoury Choux Buns

Makes about 30

150g (1 cup) vegetarian cheese
  (e.g. Cratloe, Emmental), grated
2 quantities Choux Pastry (see
  page 50)
1 egg yolk mixed with 1 tsp milk,
  for brushing

Most people associate choux pastry with sweet fillings, but these savoury buns are great as canapés or a first course.

1   Preheat the oven to 180°C/350°F/gas mark 4. Line a baking sheet with nonstick baking (parchment) paper.

2   Add 120g (4½oz) of the cheese to the glossy choux dough and stir until melted.

3   Spoon the mixture into a piping (pastry) bag fitted with a plain 1cm (½ inch) nozzle (tip). Pipe walnut-sized mounds on to the prepared baking sheet, spacing them at least 2.5cm (1 inch) apart.

4   Dip a fork into a bowl of hot water and smooth the top of each mound.

5   Brush the top of each mound with a very light coating of egg wash and sprinkle with the remaining cheese.

6   Bake for about 30 minutes, until golden brown outside and dry inside. Serve immediately, or transfer to a wire rack to cool. To reheat, warm for 3–5 minutes in an oven preheated to 180°C/350°F/gas mark 4.

Tips and ideas

•   Fill the choux with flavoured Béchamel Sauce (see page 76), or a mixture of finely chopped mushrooms and onion fried in butter.

Sauces and Stocks

Chicken Blanquette

Serves 4

Juice of 1 lemon
100g (1 cup) baby button mushrooms
50g (4 tbsp) butter
Salt and black pepper
4 boneless, skinless chicken breasts,
  about 150g (5oz) each
100ml (½ cup) white wine
1 litre (4¼ cups) White Chicken Stock
  (see page 87)
1 leek, trimmed and cut into 3 large
  pieces
1 celery stick, cut in half
1 carrot, chopped into large chunks
1 onion, studded with 1 clove
1 bouquet garni
25g (3 tbsp) plain (all-purpose) flour
300ml (1¼ cups) double (heavy)
  cream
3 egg yolks
1 tbsp Dijon mustard (optional)

To garnish
1 shallot, finely sliced
1 tsp caster (superfine) sugar

A blanquette is a ragout (stew) of chicken, veal or lamb prepared in a velouté (white) sauce. As the name suggests, it is important not to brown the meat before cooking.

1   Put half the lemon juice, the mushrooms and half the butter in a saucepan. Add salt and pepper and just enough water to cover, then bring to the boil. Leave to boil for 1 minute, then strain through a fine sieve or strainer, reserving the stock and mushrooms separately.

2   Place the chicken pieces in a large, heavy-based saucepan. Add the mushroom stock, wine and chicken stock, then the leek, celery, carrot, onion, bouquet garni and salt and pepper. Bring to the boil, skimming off any scum that rises to the surface, then cover and simmer for 30 minutes.

3   Using a slotted spoon or tongs, remove the meat from the stock and set aside with the cooked mushrooms. Cover with kitchen foil and keep warm.

4   Pass the stock through a fine sieve or strainer, discarding the solids (see tip, page 62). Measure out 500ml (2 cups) of the stock. Freeze the rest for future use.

5   To make the sauce you must start with a roux. Melt the remaining butter in a medium saucepan, stir in the flour and cook for 2½ minutes, or until lightly coloured. **(a/b)** Add the measured stock a little at a time, stirring well, then bring to the boil. **(c)** Simmer for 5 minutes, stirring occasionally until thick and smooth. **(d)**

6   Return the chicken and mushrooms to the large pan, then add the sauce and all but 1 tablespoon of the cream. Cover and simmer very gently for a further 5–10 minutes, until the chicken is cooked through.

7   Place the tablespoon of cream in a bowl with the egg yolks and mustard (if using). Beat together, then add to the sauce off the heat and stir gently. (It's important to stop the simmering or the yolks might curdle.) Add the remaining lemon juice and adjust the seasoning if necessary.

8   Finally, put the shallot and caster sugar into a dry frying pan and fry until golden brown. Sprinkle over the chicken and serve with basmati rice.

Tips and ideas

- The vegetables cooked in the stock can be served with the blanquette if you like. Just set them aside with the meat and mushrooms while preparing the sauce, then return them to the pan with the meat.

- A more economical version of this dish can be made using skinless chicken legs or thighs.

Roux Variations

A roux is a thickening agent made from equal amounts of fat and flour. It is used in three of the French mother sauces (béchamel, velouté and espagnole) and also for gravy, stews and casseroles.

The roux can be made with butter, dripping or lard, and can be cooked for different lengths of time, depending on what it will be used for:

White roux (cooked for about 2 minutes, until lightly coloured) is used for white sauce or Béchamel Sauce (see page 76).

Blond roux (cooked for about 2½ minutes, until pale brown) is perfect for velouté sauce or chicken blanquette.

Brown roux (cooked for 3 minutes, until mid-brown) is the basis of espagnole sauce and Chasseur Sauce (see page 82).

In terms of quantities, 1 litre (4¼ cups) of sauce would require 75g (6 tbsp) butter and 75g (⅔ cup) plain (all-purpose) flour to thicken it, while a stew or soup would need 40g (3 tbsp) butter and 40g (⅓ cup) flour.

Mayonnaise

Makes 300ml (1¼ cups)

2 egg yolks, preferably free-range
1 tbsp Dijon mustard, or strong
  mustard
Salt and white pepper
250ml (1 cup) sunflower oil
50ml (¼ cup) lemon juice or white
  wine vinegar

Unlike the shop-bought product, fresh mayonnaise must be used within a day or two. The flavour, though, is unbeatable.

1   Place the egg yolks, mustard and a pinch of salt and white pepper in a bowl and beat together with a balloon whisk. **(a)** Continue whisking while slowly adding the oil in a thin trickle. **(b)** As the mixture thickens, you can start adding the oil in a steadier steam.

2   When the mayonnaise is thick and glossy, add the lemon juice, then taste and adjust the seasoning if necessary. **(c/d)** Cover and store in the refrigerator until required.

Tips and ideas

- Take the eggs from the refrigerator an hour or so beforehand to bring them to room temperature.

Mayonnaise Variations

Curry Mayonnaise Sauce – mix 100g (½ cup) mayonnaise with 1 tsp red curry paste or 1 tbsp mild curry powder.

Herb Pesto Mayonnaise – combine 100g (½ cup) mayonnaise with 2 tbsp ready-made herb pesto and the juice of ½ lemon.

Marie-Rose Sauce – combine 100g (½ cup) mayonnaise with 2 tbsp tomato ketchup, 1 tsp tomato purée (paste), 1 tsp Worcestershire sauce, a few drops of Tabasco and 3 tbsp brandy.

Ranch Dressing – combine 100g (½ cup) mayonnaise with 1 tbsp chopped parsley, 1 small chopped garlic clove, 2 dashes of Worcestershire sauce, a dash of Tabasco, 120ml (½ cup) buttermilk, and salt and pepper.

Tartare Sauce – see page 148.

a

b

c

d

Simple Coleslaw

Serves 6

½ head of green cabbage, shredded
2 carrots, grated
1 onion or 2 shallots, thinly sliced
250g (1¼ cups) Mayonnaise (see
  page 64)
1 tbsp lemon juice
1 tbsp English mustard paste
Salt and black pepper

Cabbage is a great source of vitamins, minerals and fibre, especially when eaten raw. It's really tasty and satisfying in this simple recipe.

1   Place the cabbage, carrots and onion in a large bowl and toss together.

2   Combine the mayonnaise, lemon juice and mustard in a separate bowl, then add to vegetables. Season with salt and pepper, toss gently and serve straight away.

Tips and ideas

• If making this recipe in advance, dress the coleslaw just before serving so that the cabbage and carrots stay crunchy.

• If you want to remove excess water from the shredded cabbage, place it in a colander, sprinkle with salt and set aside for a few hours. Rinse and drain, then use as required.

• For a lighter coleslaw, use yogurt instead of mayonnaise to make the dressing.

Vinaigrette

Serves 4

1 tsp Dijon mustard
Pinch of caster (superfine) sugar
 (optional)
Salt and black pepper
2 tbsp white wine vinegar
6 tbsp sunflower oil

A successful vinaigrette depends on getting the right proportions of oil, vinegar and mustard to make a smooth emulsion. Follow this recipe and you won't go wrong.

1   Place the mustard and sugar (if using) in a bowl and season with salt and pepper. Whisk to combine. **(a)** Continue whisking while adding the vinegar and then the oil. **(b/c)** Taste and adjust the seasoning if necessary.

2   Store in a Kilner or screwtop jar and shake well before using. **(d)**

Vinaigrette Variations

Once you have mastered the basic vinaigrette, you can customize it to suit just about any meal. There are lots of flavoured oils and vinegars to experiment with, and you could try adding honey, sugar or fruit juice to achieve the flavour you desire. Also, try some of the following ideas:

Balsamic Dressing – combine 1 tbsp balsamic vinegar with 3 tbsp olive oil, salt and pepper.

Creamy Garlic and Anchovy Dressing – pound 1 finely chopped garlic clove and 2 anchovy fillets to a paste and add it to the basic vinaigrette.

Creamy Vinaigrette Dressing – add 2 tbsp crème fraîche to the basic vinaigrette.

Lemon Dressing – combine the juice of ½ lemon with 3 tbsp extra virgin olive oil, salt and pepper.

Parmesan and Black Pepper Dressing – add 20g (¼ cup) grated Parmesan cheese and freshly ground black pepper to taste.

a

b

c

d

Courgette and Feta Pasta Salad

Serves 4

450g (1lb) farfalle pasta or similar
Salt and black pepper
2 tbsp olive oil
4 courgettes (zucchini), peeled into
   ribbons
400g (2⅔ cups) feta cheese, crumbled
1 tbsp chopped flat leaf parsley
1 tbsp snipped chives
1 tbsp chopped mint
Zest and juice of 1 lemon
2–3 tbsp Vinaigrette (see page 68)

This is a lovely light salad that tastes of summer. If making it for vegetarians, you can use vegetarian feta, which is guaranteed to contain no rennet.

1   Bring a large saucepan of salted water to the boil, and cook the pasta until al dente. Drain and rinse under cold running water, then set aside.

2   Place a griddle (ridged grill) pan over a high heat and drizzle in the oil. When hot, add the strips of courgette a few at a time, season with salt and pepper and cook on each side for 1–2 minutes. Transfer to a large bowl as they are cooked.

3   Add the pasta, feta, herbs and lemon zest, drizzle with the lemon juice and vinaigrette and season with salt and pepper. Serve immediately.

Tips and ideas

- Add chopped olives or shallots for extra texture.

- Pan-frying the courgette ribbons in small batches will keep them greener and make them crisper.

Béarnaise Sauce

Serves 6

1 small shallot, very finely diced
½ tsp white wine vinegar
2 egg yolks
250g (2¼ sticks) clarified butter
  (see page 16)
Salt and white pepper
2 tsp chopped tarragon

Although traditionally served with red meat, Béarnaise sauce is also used with other dishes, such as roast lamb, pork or chicken. There are several ways to make the sauce, but I find the following method works best. Just be careful not to overheat the bowl or the eggs will scramble.

1   Bring a saucepan of water to the boil, then reduce the heat and keep it on a very gentle simmer.

2   Put the shallot and vinegar into a heatproof bowl set over the pan of simmering water, making sure the bottom of the bowl does not touch the water. Leave to infuse for a minute or two, then add the egg yolks and whisk constantly until the colour lightens and the mixture thickens (about 5 minutes). **(a)** You will need to move the bowl (not the pan) on and off the heat as you whisk to prevent the eggs scrambling. **(b)**

3   Slowly add the clarified butter, whisking constantly. **(c)** Taste the sauce, season with salt and white pepper if necessary and add the chopped tarragon. **(d)**

4   Serve immediately, or keep warm in a china teapot or heatproof jug (pitcher) set in warm water.

Tips and ideas

- To rescue a split sauce, put 2 tsp mayonnaise in a clean bowl and gradually beat in the curdled mixture.

Béarnaise Sauce Variations

Choron Sauce – add 1 tbsp tomato purée (paste) to the basic sauce and serve with white meats.

Paloise Sauce – use mint instead of tarragon for a sauce that goes perfectly with lamb.

a

b

c

d

Seared Fillet of Beef with Mushrooms, Onions and Béarnaise Sauce

Serves 4

4 fillets of beef (beef tenderloins),
  about 175–200g (6–7oz) each
3 tbsp rapeseed (canola) oil
Salt and black pepper
100g (1 stick) butter
1 onion, thinly sliced
2 garlic cloves, crushed
12–14 mushrooms, thinly sliced
1 quantity Béarnaise Sauce, to serve
  (see page 72)

I like to use fillet steak in this dish because it is so tender. Béarnaise sauce is a perfect accompaniment to this dish.

1   Heat a frying pan until smoking hot.

2   Brush the fillets with a little oil and place in the pan. Season with salt and pepper and cook for about 2–3 minutes on one side, then 2 minutes on the other. Reduce the heat to medium and add the butter. When foaming, spoon it over the meat for just a few moments, then transfer the fillets to a warm plate while you cook the vegetables.

3   Add the onion, garlic and mushrooms to the empty pan and fry over a medium heat for 3–5 minutes, until caramelized.

4   Serve the meat and vegetables with creamy garlic mashed potatoes and Béarnaise sauce.

Tips and ideas

• Add 1 tbsp cold water to the pan if the butter starts to brown too quickly. This will cool it down and give the beef a few extra minutes to cook.

Béchamel Sauce

Serves 4

25g (2 tbsp) butter
25g (3 tbsp) plain (all-purpose) flour
500ml (2 cups) milk
Salt and white pepper

Béchamel is a white sauce, and the basis of many other sauces. It's perfect with poultry, pork or ham. Any leftover sauce can be stored in an airtight container in the refrigerator for up to 4 days.

1   Melt the butter in a heavy-based saucepan over a low heat. **(a)** Sprinkle in the flour and stir with a balloon whisk. Cook gently for 2 minutes, until the roux is off-white in colour. **(b)** Take care not to overcook it as this will make the sauce discoloured.

2   Slowly pour the milk on to the roux and increase the heat to medium, whisking constantly until it comes to the boil. **(c)** Season with salt and white pepper and cook for a further 6–8 minutes to ensure the flour is cooked through. **(d)**

Tips and ideas

- For extra flavour, infuse the milk before use. Simply add a clove-studded onion and a bay leaf to it, bring to the boil and simmer for a few minutes. Remove the onion and bay leaf, then use the milk as required.

- If you are not using the sauce right away, add a knob or pat of butter to it to prevent a skin forming.

Béchamel Sauce Variations

Cheese Sauce – add 100g (1 cup) grated Cheddar.

Mornay Sauce – add 70g (¾ cup) grated Gruyère and 1 egg yolk to the sauce.

Parsley Sauce – add 2 tbsp chopped parsley to the sauce.

Tomato Sauce

**Makes 750ml–1.5 litres (3–6 cups),
depending on thickness required**

3kg (7lb) very ripe plump tomatoes,
cored and a cross scored on the
bottom
65ml (4 tbsp plus 1 tsp) red wine
vinegar, or to taste
2 tsp salt
2 tsp brown sugar (optional)

Best made at the end of the summer, when
tomatoes are full of flavour, this is a very
versatile sauce. Keep it thin for coating pasta,
or reduce it for enriching soups and stews.

1   Bring a large saucepan of water to the boil. Meanwhile,
fill a large bowl with water and ice and place it beside
the hob or stove.

2   Drop several tomatoes at a time into the boiling water
and leave them until you see the skin starting to wrinkle
and split, about 45–60 seconds. **(a)** Lift out with a
slotted spoon and plunge them into the iced water. **(b)**
When cool, transfer them to another bowl. Repeat this
step with the remaining tomatoes.

3   Peel the tomatoes, then roughly chop the flesh. **(c/d)**
Working in batches, pulse them in a blender or food
processor to the consistency you prefer – either chunky
or smooth. **(e)**

4   Transfer the tomatoes to a large saucepan and bring
to a simmer over a medium-low heat. Cook, uncovered,
for 30–40 minutes, stirring occasionally, until the sauce
reaches the taste and consistency that you like. **(f)** Stir
in the vinegar and salt. Taste and add some brown sugar
if the sauce is a little sharp.

5   Store for up to a week in the refrigerator, or pot up in
sterilized screwtop jars (see tip) – it will keep for a few
months, stored in the freezer in hot regions.

Tomato Sauce Variation

Flavoured Tomato Sauce – blanch, peel and chop 1kg (2¼lb)
tomatoes as above. Heat 2 tbsp olive oil in a heavy-based
saucepan. Add 1 finely chopped onion, carrot and celery stick
plus 2 tbsp chopped parsley, then cover and cook over a
low heat for 10–12 minutes, stirring occasionally, until the
vegetables are soft. Add 3 chopped garlic cloves and cook for
30 seconds over a medium-high heat. Add the tomatoes and
their juice, 1 tsp tomato purée (paste) and 2 tbsp chopped basil.
Season with salt and pepper to taste, adding a pinch of chilli
if you like, then simmer, uncovered, until thickened – about
15 minutes. If you want a smooth sauce, blend it with a hand
blender. Store in the same way as Tomato Sauce (see above).

Tips and ideas

- To sterilize jars and their lids, wash
on the hottest cycle in a dishwasher.
Alternatively, wash thoroughly, then
place upside down in a very low
oven for 30 minutes. Fill them while
still warm.

Beef Lasagne

Serves 4

6 sheets of lasagne
500ml (2 cups) Béchamel Sauce
(see page 76)
300g (2⅔ cups) Cheddar cheese,
grated

For the beef sauce
Olive oil
1 carrot, finely chopped
1 celery stick, finely chopped
1 onion, finely chopped
2 garlic cloves, crushed
750g (1½lb) minced (ground) beef
20g (1 rounded tbsp) tomato purée
(paste)
150ml (⅔ cup) red wine
200ml (1 cup) beef stock
400g (1⅔ cups) Tomato Sauce
(see page 78)
1 tsp mixed fresh herbs
Salt and black pepper

a

b

Layers of meaty sauce with cheese and béchamel sauce, topped with more glorious cheese – it is little wonder that lasagne is a real family favourite, especially with my daughter Sophie. The lasagne sheets do not need precooking.

1   Heat a little olive oil in a large frying pan and sauté the carrot, celery, onion and garlic for 3–5 minutes, until cooked but not completely soft.

2   Add the minced beef, mix thoroughly and cook until it is browned.

3   Stir in the tomato purée, red wine and stock and cook gently, uncovered, for 2 minutes.

4   Add the tomato sauce and herbs and cook for 10–15 minutes, until most of the liquid has reduced. Season with salt and pepper to taste. **(a)**

5   Preheat the oven to 180°C/350°F/gas mark 4.

6   Place a layer of the meat sauce in the bottom of a 25 x 18cm (10 x 8 inch) baking dish. Add a layer of the pasta, a layer of béchamel and sprinkle with some of the grated cheese. **(b)** Repeat these layers, finishing with béchamel and grated cheese. Bake for 35–40 minutes, until bubbling hot.

7   Serve with a crisp green salad and garlic bread.

Tips and ideas

• Try adding 100g (½ cup) ricotta cheese to the basic béchamel for a richer flavour.

• The sautéd mixture of chopped carrots, celery and onions is known as *mirepoix*, and is used to add flavour to stocks, sauces and other dishes. It usually consists of 50 per cent onion, 25 per cent carrot and 25 per cent celery.

Chicken with Chasseur Sauce

Serves 4

4 boneless chicken breasts, with
   skin on, about 150g (5oz) each
Salt and black pepper

For the sauce
75g (6 tbsp) butter, cubed
3 shallots, finely chopped
120g (1¾ cups) button mushrooms,
   sliced
1 tbsp brandy
1 tbsp plain (all-purpose) flour
200ml (1 cup) dry white wine
150ml (⅔ cup) hot reduced White
   Chicken Stock (see page 87)
1 tsp tomato purée (paste)
2 tomatoes, chopped
1 tbsp chopped parsley
1 tbsp chopped tarragon

Chasseur (hunter's) sauce is based on a *demi-glace*, which is made by slowly simmering stock, aromatics and wine into a concentrated, intensely flavoured glaze. This is the foundation for many sauces and gravies, and is fantastic for enhancing soups, stews and risottos. The chasseur variation works extremely well with poultry or veal.

1   Preheat the oven to 180°C/350°F/gas mark 4.

2   Season the chicken breasts with salt and pepper. Place a flameproof, ovenproof frying pan over a medium heat. When hot, fry the breasts, skin-side down, for 2 minutes, or until the skin has browned. Turn the breasts flesh-side down and place in the oven for 15 minutes, or until cooked through. **(a)** Transfer the chicken to a plate, cover with kitchen foil and keep warm while making the sauce. **(b)**

3   Being careful not to burn your hand on the handle of the empty pan, place it over a medium-low heat and melt 50g (4 tbsp) of the butter in it until foaming. **(c)** Add the shallots and mushrooms and stir gently for 2 minutes, or until the mushrooms are tender. **(d)** Drizzle in the brandy, then carefully set it alight to burn off the alcohol. When the flames have gone out, add the flour and stir with a wooden spoon for 2 minutes, or until browned. **(e)**

4   Pour in the wine and stir well to deglaze the pan, scraping up any bits from the base of the pan, and smooth out any lumps. **(f)** Add the stock, tomato purée, chopped tomatoes, parsley and tarragon, increase the heat to medium and bring to the boil, stirring constantly. **(g)** Reduce the heat and simmer, stirring, for 3–5 minutes, or until the sauce thickens slightly and coats the back of a spoon. Taste and season with salt and pepper if necessary.

5   Remove from the heat and stir in the remaining butter to finish the sauce.

6   Return the chicken to the pan and spoon the sauce over it. **(h)** Serve immediately.

e

f

g

h

Beef Stock

Makes about 2 litres (8½ cups)

1kg (2¼lb) beef bones
3 large carrots, roughly
  chopped
2 celery sticks, roughly
  chopped
1 onion, roughly chopped
2 bay leaves
3 sprigs of rosemary
3 sprigs of flat leaf parsley
2–3 litres (8½–12⅔ cups)
  cold water

1   Preheat the oven to
    180°C/350°F/gas mark 4.

2   Place the beef bones in a
    large roasting pan and roast
    for up to 1 hour, until they
    are well browned.

3   Transfer the bones to a
    large saucepan, add the
    carrots, celery, onion, bay
    leaves and herbs and cover
    with water. Bring to the boil,
    then simmer, uncovered,
    for 2 hours, skimming off
    any scum that rises to
    the surface.

4   Strain the stock through a
    muslin (cheesecloth)-lined
    colander into a large jug
    (pitcher) or bowl, discarding
    the solids. Leave to cool,
    preferably overnight. The
    next morning you can
    simply lift off and discard
    the fat, which will have
    solidified on the top.

5   Cover with clingfilm (plastic
    wrap) and store in the
    refrigerator for up to 2 days.

Fish Stock

Makes about 2 litres (8½ cups)

2 onions, chopped
1 leek, trimmed and
  roughly chopped
1 carrot, chopped
1 celery stick, chopped
2 garlic cloves, unpeeled
100ml (½ cup) olive oil
1.5kg (3¼lb) white fish bones
  and heads, well rinsed and
  roughly chopped
2 litres (8½ cups) water
2 sprigs each of tarragon, flat
  leaf parsley and thyme, tied
  together with string
½ lemon, sliced
Salt and black pepper

1   Place the onions, leek,
    carrot, celery and garlic
    in a large saucepan. Add
    the oil and heat until the
    vegetables start to sizzle.
    Cover and gently sweat
    them over a low heat for
    about 15 minutes, until
    softened but not coloured.

2   Add the fish bones and
    heads, then pour in the
    water. Stir in the herbs,
    lemon and seasoning. Bring
    to the boil, skimming off
    any scum that rises to the
    surface, then simmer,
    uncovered, for 20 minutes.
    Leave to stand for at least
    10 minutes to allow the
    flavours to infuse.

3   Strain the stock through a
    muslin (cheesecloth)-lined
    colander into a large jug
    (pitcher) or bowl, discarding
    the solids. Leave to cool.

4   Cover with clingfilm (plastic
    wrap) and store in the
    refrigerator for up to 2 days.

Brown Chicken Stock

Makes about 2 litres (8½ cups)

2kg (4½lb) chicken thighs,
  wings or raw carcasses,
  roughly chopped
2–3 sprigs each of thyme,
  tarragon and oregano
4 litres (17 cups) water
2 onions, roughly chopped
2 leeks, trimmed and roughly
  chopped
2 celery sticks, roughly
  chopped
2 carrots, roughly chopped
½ garlic bulb, cut horizontally
2 tsp sea salt

1   Preheat the oven to
    200°C/400°F/gas mark 6.

2   Place the chicken pieces or
    carcasses in a large roasting
    pan and roast for 15–20
    minutes, turning them once
    or twice, until dark golden.

3   Transfer the bones to a large
    saucepan. Add the herbs and
    water and bring to the boil,
    skimming off any scum that
    rises to the surface. Add the
    remaining ingredients and
    bring back to the boil, then
    simmer, uncovered, for 3
    hours, skimming occasionally.

4   Taste the stock and adjust
    the seasoning if necessary.
    Strain the stock through a
    muslin (cheesecloth)-lined
    colander into a large jug
    (pitcher) or bowl, discarding
    the solids. Leave to cool.

5   Cover with clingfilm (plastic
    wrap) and store in the
    refrigerator for up to 2 days.

White Chicken Stock

Makes 1 litre (4¼ cups)

2 raw chicken carcasses, quartered and excess fat removed
2–3 litres (8½–12⅔ cups) cold water
1 onion, roughly chopped
1 celery stick, roughly chopped
1 bay leaf
2 sprigs of thyme
¼ tsp whole black peppercorns
Small handful of parsley stems

1 Place the chicken carcasses in a large saucepan, cover with water and bring to the boil. Simmer for 3 minutes, skimming off any scum and fat that rise to the surface. Drain, discarding the water.

2 Return the carcasses to the empty pan, add all the remaining ingredients into the large stockpot and bring to a light simmer and simmer, uncovered, for 2–3 hours, skimming off any scum that rises to the surface.

3 Strain the stock through a muslin (cheesecloth)-lined colander into a large jug (pitcher) or bowl, discarding the solids.

4 Cover with clingfilm (plastic wrap) and store in the refrigerator for up to 2 days.

Vegetable Stock

Makes about 2 litres (8½ cups)

3 onions, roughly chopped
1 leek, trimmed and roughly chopped
2 celery sticks, roughly chopped
1 garlic bulb, cut in half horizontally
6 carrots, roughly chopped
¼ tsp white peppercorns
¼ tsp black peppercorns
1 small bay leaf
2–3 sprigs each of basil, coriander (cilantro), thyme, flat leaf parsley and tarragon, tied together with string
Pinch of salt
2 litres (8½ cups) water

1 Place the onions, leek, celery, garlic and carrots in a large saucepan. Add the peppercorns, herbs and salt. Pour in the water and bring to the boil, then simmer, uncovered, for 10 minutes. Set aside until completely cold.

2 Transfer the contents of the pan to a large jug or bowl, cover with clingfilm (plastic wrap) and place in the refrigerator for 24 hours.

3 Strain the stock through a muslin (cheesecloth)-lined colander into a large jug (pitcher) or bowl, discarding the solids.

4 Cover with clingfilm (plastic wrap) and store in the refrigerator for up to 2 days.

Tips and ideas

- Freeze stock in ice-cube trays, then transfer them to freezer bags for storage. Use within 2 months.

- For a more concentrated flavour to use as a base for sauces, simmer the strained Fish Stock until reduced by half.

- For a stronger jellied Brown Chicken Stock, boil the strained stock until reduced by half.

- White Chicken Stock is a clear and lightly fragrant stock, perfect for adding subtle flavouring to a variety of soups and other dishes.

- Do not allow the White Chicken Stock to boil, or the fat and scum will mix with it and cause it to become cloudy.

- Try adding a splash of wine to the Vegetable Stock for an even more intense flavour.

Broccoli Soup

Serves 4

2 tbsp olive oil
1 onion, finely diced
1 garlic clove, finely chopped
2–3 sprigs of thyme
Salt and black pepper
750ml (3 cups) hot Vegetable Stock
(see page 87)
1 head of broccoli, cut into small florets
1 potato, very finely chopped
100ml (½ cup) double (heavy) cream,
plus extra to serve (optional)

My cousin Pippa gave me the recipe for this delicious soup, which is super-quick and easy to prepare. You can add a pinch of nutmeg, if you like, and top it with crumbled feta cheese. This recipe was a particular favourite of Pippa's son Kieran, who sadly passed away, and I often think of him when I make this soup.

1 Place the oil in a saucepan over a medium heat. When hot, add the onion, garlic, thyme and salt and pepper. Cook for 3–4 minutes, until the onion is translucent.

2 Pour in the stock and bring to the boil, then add the broccoli and potato and bring to the boil again. Reduce the heat and simmer for 15–20 minutes. **(a)**

3 Pour in the cream, then taste and adjust the seasoning if necessary. Using a hand blender, blend the soup until a smooth consistency is achieved. **(b)**

4 Serve immediately, with an extra dash of cream if you like.

a

b

Tips and ideas

- Chop the broccoli into bite-sized pieces so it will cook quickly and retain its colour, vitamins and fibre.

- Add some chorizo or smoked bacon with the onions to add a meaty flavour.

- Use cauliflower, cabbage or parsnips instead of the broccoli if you like.

Meat

Cooking Meat

This chapter covers beef, lamb, pork and offal or variety meats, all of which Ireland produces in large amounts and is of great quality.

Beef

Irish beef is considered among the best in the world because the animals feed on lush grass for most of the year. I like to buy my beef after it has been hung for a minimum of 21 days, because this gives time for the enzymes in the meat to break down the fibres, making for more tender and flavoursome cuts. When buying beef, look for a ruby red colour with some creamy-white fat marbling through the meat, which helps with the basting during the cooking process.

Beef cuts for roasting

The best cut of beefs for roasting in the oven are sirloin or striploin, top rib and fillet (tenderloin).

Leave the meat to come up to room temperature for a few hours before you plan to roast it so that the cooking time will be more accurate. Also, take care not to oversalt the beef when seasoning, because salt draws out the juices and can cause dryness.

Use a roasting pan that is just a little bigger than your meat. If an overlarge tin is used, the juices will spread out and burn, which is not a good thing because you need them to make your gravy.

It is important to leave the meat to rest before serving so that the fibres relax and the juices are retained. If meat is cut into straight after cooking, a pool of juices would spill on to the plate The optimum resting times are about 5 minutes for steak, and 20–25 minutes for a roast joint. In both cases, rest the meat under a kitchen foil tent to keep it warm.

Beef cuts for stewing, braising or pot-roasting

The best cuts of beef for long, slow cooking are topside, silverside (bottom round roast), brisket, short ribs, shin (shank), cheek and chuck steak. They tend to be a little tougher than other cuts, so the longer cooking time ensures they become tender. In fact, all benefit from being cooked the day before, then reheated when required. Silverside and brisket are also suitable for salting and boiling.

Beef cuts for pan-frying

The best steaks for cooking on a griddle (ridged grill pan) or in a frying pan are rib-eye, fillet and striploin, T-bone and sirloin.

Buy a steak at least 2–3cm (¾–1¼ inches) thick and leave to come to room temperature for at least an hour before cooking. Heat your pan until it's smoking hot, then add the steak and try not to move it until it's brown and caramelized on the underside. Turn it over and cook the other side until it's a similar colour.

Lamb

Like most Irish meat, lamb is reared on the country's lush grass, so it is of high quality and very popular, especially in springtime. The animals have to be marketed within a year of their birth to be called 'lamb'. Anything older is known as 'mutton'. Early season lamb is tender, and therefore widely used for roasting. Older meat, though, has a more pronounced flavour and works better in stews and casseroles.

Lamb cuts for roasting

Many parts of lamb are great for roasting, including leg, rack, saddle, shoulder and best end of neck.

For an impressive dish when entertaining, two racks of lamb can be brought together in a circle to make a 'crown'. If you don't want to be bothered with bones, try noisettes of lamb, which are made from a boned and rolled loin.

Lamb can be flavoured during roasting by inserting slivers of garlic, tiny sprigs of rosemary or pieces of anchovy in small incisions in the skin. Marinades and rubs work very well too.

As with all meats, leave the meat to rest before carving. This allows the fibres to relax and retain the juices. Simply cover loosely with kitchen foil – not tightly or the meat will sweat and lose valuable moisture – and rest for 20–25 minutes.

Lamb cuts for stewing

The best lamb cuts for slow cooking are shanks and the neck (boneless shoulder). However, do ensure the heat is not too high. The lamb should simmer gently to prevent the excess fat from emulsifying with the sauce and creating a greasy stew. If cooked gently, the fat can simply be skimmed off at the end of the cooking process.

Lamb cooks more quickly than other meat, so check it after about 45 minutes and you may find it is already tender enough to eat.

Lamb cuts for pan-frying

The most popular cuts for frying or griddling are cutlets, chops and chump steaks.

Ideally, you want to achieve crispy fat on chops, so use tongs to hold it in contact with the pan.

Pork

The pig is a fantastic source of meat. Apart from being used fresh, it can also be cured to provide ham, gammon (cured ham steak) and bacon, or minced (ground) and made into sausages.

Pork cuts for roasting

The best cuts for roasting include loin, spare ribs, chump chops, best end cutlets and fillet (tenderloin).

If storing a pork joint or roast before cooking, cover it loosely with nonstick baking (parchment) paper and place in the refrigerator. This allows the skin to dry slightly, which will ultimately produce better crackling.

To cook a perfect pork roast with crunchy crackling, score the skin with a very sharp knife and rub with oil and sea salt. Place it in an oven preheated to 240°C/475°F/gas mark 9 for the first 15–20 minutes, then reduce the heat to 180°C/350°F/gas mark 4 and cook for 20 minutes per 450g (1lb).

I like pork to be cooked to medium because overcooking can make it tough and dry. When it's ready, leave in the roasting pan, loosely covered with kitchen foil, and leave to rest for 20–25 minutes.

Pork cuts for stewing and braising

The best cuts for slow cooking are the belly, shanks and trotters (feet). It is not necessary to remove excess fat from these cuts because the slow cooking process simply melts it and keeps the meat juicy. Any scum that comes to the surface can be removed with a ladle.

Cooking the pork in flavoured liquid, such as good stock and/or wine, will enhance the flavour of the meat and make it meltingly tender.

Offal

The internal parts of an animal known as 'offal' (variety meats) tend to be cheaper than other cuts. Those most common are the kidneys, liver, heart, sweetbreads and sometimes the tongue.

Fresh offal should be firm, juicy and moist without a strong odour. Kidneys and liver should be either quickly pan-fried or added to pie fillings; hearts can be stuffed and braised or pan-fried; and sweetbreads are delicious coated in breadcrumbs and pan-fried in butter. Tongue is best if brined (soaked in a salt solution) and poached, after which it can be eaten hot or cold.

Storing and freezing meat

As soon as you get your meat home, remove any plastic packaging because it makes meat sweat, then transfer it to a plate and cover loosely with kitchen foil or clingfilm (plastic wrap). If not using your meat straight away, store in the refrigerator and use within 3 days, unless the wrapping states otherwise. Use cooked meat within 5 days.

If you decide to freeze your meat, uncooked joints or roasts can be stored for up to 6 months. Minced (ground) meat and small cuts, such as chops, should be used within 3 months.

Do not refreeze defrosted meat unless it has been cooked because it impairs the flavour and texture.

Glazed Rack of Bacon Ribs

Serves 4-6

1 onion, chopped
1 carrot, chopped
2 bay leaves
2-3 sprigs of thyme
Salt and black pepper
2 large racks of bacon ribs
2 tbsp Irish whiskey marmalade
  (ordinary marmalade will suffice)
2 tbsp water
Dried chilli flakes (optional)

Ribs are delicious finger food, great to enjoy at any time. Look for ribs that have meat covering the entire length of the bones. Allow 6 baby ribs per person, or 3 standard ribs.

1   Preheat the oven to 180°C/350°F/gas mark 4.

2   Half-fill a deep roasting pan with water, then add the onion, carrot, herbs and salt and pepper. Place a wire rack over the pan, sit the ribs on it and cover with kitchen foil. **(a)** Roast for 40-45 minutes.

3   Meanwhile, heat the marmalade in a small saucepan and add the water.

4   When the first roasting period is over, remove the foil from the ribs and pat dry with kitchen paper (paper towels). Brush the marmalade glaze over them, and add a sprinkling of chilli flakes too, if you like a spicy kick to your ribs. **(b)** Return to the oven for 35-40 minutes, turning occasionally. Serve immediately.

a

b

Tips and ideas

• When cooking ribs, keep the rack together – don't cut into individual portions.

• If you have any leftover meat, remove it from the bones and use in a sandwich.

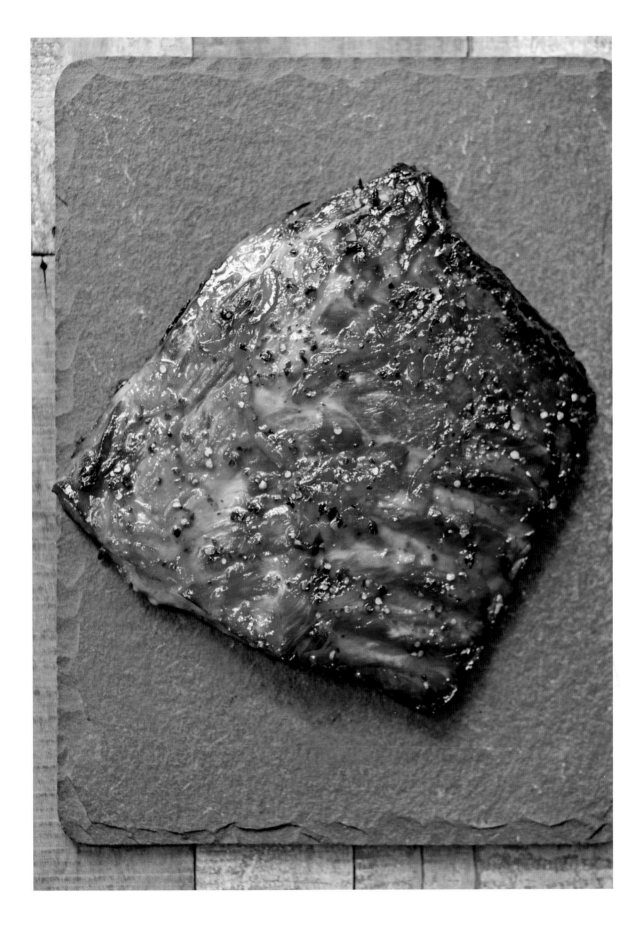

Navarin of Lamb

Serves 6

50ml (¼ cup) olive oil
50g (4 tbsp) butter
1kg (2¼lb) shoulder of lamb, diced
Salt and black pepper
100ml (½ cup) brandy
2 tbsp cornflour (cornstarch)
2 onions, sliced
4 carrots, diced
200g (7oz) young turnips, chopped
4 garlic cloves, crushed
1 tsp rosemary leaves
1 bay leaf
50ml (¼ cup) sherry vinegar
2 tbsp tomato purée (paste)
500ml (2 cups) lamb stock or
   Beef Stock (see page 86)
300g (5 cups) mangetout (snow peas)
1 tbsp roughly chopped parsley, to
   serve

a

b

This is a traditional French dish of braised lamb and vegetables, which is similar to a light stew. Using shoulder lamb makes this an economical dish, which is great if you're feeding a family. Any leftovers can be reheated and eaten the next day, as the flavour improves.

1   Preheat the oven to 180°C/350°F/gas mark 4.

2   Heat the oil and butter in a large frying pan and brown the lamb in batches, seasoning well with salt and pepper. **(a)** Transfer to an ovenproof casserole dish.

3   Discard the excess oil from the pan, then return the lamb to it and add the brandy. Place over a high heat to evaporate, then sprinkle in the cornflour and stir to coat the lamb. **(b)** Return the meat to the casserole dish and add the onions, carrots, turnips, garlic, rosemary and bay.

4   Put the vinegar, tomato purée and stock into a clean saucepan and bring to the boil over a high heat. Pour the liquid over the meat mixture, stir well and cover.

5   Bake for 1½–1¾ hours, until the lamb is tender, adding the mangetout 10 minutes before the end of the cooking time. Taste and adjust the seasoning if necessary, then scatter the chopped parsley over just before serving.

Tips and ideas

•   Braising, also known as pot-roasting, is similar to stewing, but has one fundamental difference: braising requires oven cooking for a while, whereas stewing is done on the hob or stove.

Lambs' Liver with Red Wine Gravy

Serves 4

500g (18oz) lambs' liver, cut into
   4 portions
2 tbsp plain (all-purpose) flour
Salt and black pepper
2 tbsp olive oil
50g (4 tbsp) butter
2 onions, thinly sliced
1 tsp finely chopped sage
250ml (1 cup) Beef Stock
   (see page 86)
150ml (⅔ cup) red wine

Liver is widely underrated and deserves to be eaten more often. Apart from being rich in iron and vitamin A, it cooks in just a few minutes and can be deliciously flavoured with herbs, sage being the most usual option. Liver and onions is a classic combination, and the onions here are incorporated into the gravy.

1   Rinse the liver thoroughly under cold running water and pat dry with kitchen paper (paper towels).

2   Place the flour in a shallow dish and season with salt and pepper. Dip the liver in the flour, coating it all over and patting gently to remove any excess. **(a)**

3   Put the oil and half the butter in a frying pan over a medium heat. When the butter has melted, cook the liver for 1–2 minutes on each side. It should still be slightly pink in the middle. **(b)** Transfer to a plate and keep warm, then fry the onions and sage for 2–3 minutes.

4   Pour the stock and wine into the pan and bring to the boil. Continue boiling until reduced by half, or until the liquid coats the back of a spoon. Remove from the heat, add the remaining butter and stir until incorporated.

5   Return the liver to the pan and coat with the sauce. Serve immediately with some creamy mashed potatoes.

a

b

Tips and ideas

- Liver cooks so quickly, and turns leathery if cooked too long, that it's a good idea to cook whatever you plan to serve with it before you start cooking the liver itself.

- Use fresh rather than frozen liver for this recipe, either lamb or beef. If you like, you can soak it in milk for about 15 minutes before cooking to remove any bitterness.

- Try lambs' liver in a stroganoff sauce, with mushrooms, onions, white wine and crème fraîche. Alternatively, fry with crushed peppercorns, deglazed with sherry vinegar and butter – delicious!

Pork Fillet with Black Olive Tapenade and Tagliatelle

Serves 4

3 tbsp olive oil
2 pork fillets (tenderloins), about 450g (1lb) each, trimmed and cut in half
25g (2 tbsp) butter
3 shallots, finely chopped
2 tbsp sherry
500ml (2 cups) Brown Chicken Stock (see page 86)
Salt and black pepper
1 tsp chopped thyme
450g (1lb) tagliatelle (see page 20 if using fresh pasta)
1 tsp chopped flat leaf parsley

For the tapenade
250g (2½ cups) black olives, pitted
3 garlic cloves
150ml (⅔ cup) olive oil, plus extra for drizzling and storing
Juice of ½ lemon
1 tbsp chopped walnuts
3-4 canned anchovy fillets

Tips and ideas

- To add additional flavour to the pork, brush a glaze over it after sealing but before cooking it in the oven. You could try barbecue sauce or a *demi-glace*, such as Chasseur Sauce (see page 82).

- If you are entertaining and need to serve up quickly, cut your fillet into medallions and sauté them in foaming butter and a dash of brandy for 2–3 minutes on each side. Finish with a splash of cream.

When trimming the pork fillet, it's important to remove all the sinew to prevent the meat from curling up while cooking. Tapenade is a very simple olive paste, delicious to have on hand to add a touch of the Mediterranean to your life.

1 First make the tapenade. Put all the ingredients for it into a blender or food processor and blend for 2-3 minutes, until smooth. If you would like to make the paste a little looser, you can add an extra drizzle of olive oil.

2 Spoon the tapenade into a bowl **(a)** or transfer to a sterilized jar (see page 78) and pour 3-4 teaspoons olive oil over the top. Seal tightly and store in the refrigerator for up to 7 days.

3 Preheat the oven to 180°C/350°F/gas mark 4.

4 Heat 1 tablespoon of the oil in an ovenproof frying pan. Add the pork fillets and half the butter and cook over a medium heat until the meat is brown all over. **(b)** Transfer the pork to a plate, cover with kitchen foil and keep warm. **(c)**

5 Melt the remaining butter in the empty pan, add the shallots and sauté gently. Add the sherry and allow to evaporate, then pour in the stock. **(d)** Season with a little salt and pepper, bring to the boil, then simmer for 5-8 minutes until reduced by half. **(e)** Stir in 2 tablespoons of the tapenade and the thyme. **(f/g)**

6 Lay the pork fillets in the pan of sauce and bake for 15-20 minutes. **(h)**

7 Meanwhile, bring a large saucepan of salted water to the boil and cook the tagliatelle until al dente. Drain, then coat with the remaining oil.

8 Cut the pork into diagonal slices and serve on a bed of pasta sprinkled with parsley and drizzled with the sauce.

Roast Beef with Yorkshire Puddings, Roast Potatoes and Gravy

Serves 4–6

3 carrots, cut into chunks
1 large onion, cut into chunks
1 garlic bulb
About 2kg (4½lb) sirloin (tenderloin)
   of beef
Sunflower oil, for roasting

For the Yorkshire puddings
250g (2 cups) plain (all-purpose) flour
Salt and black pepper
4 eggs, beaten
400ml (1⅔ cups) milk

For the roast potatoes
8–12 potatoes
50g (¼ cup) duck fat or oil

For the gravy
1 tbsp plain flour
85ml (⅓ cup) red wine
300ml (1¼ cups) Beef Stock (see
   page 86)

There's nothing nicer than sharing a home-cooked roast with family and friends, especially if light and airy (popover-like) Yorkshire puddings are part of the meal. For the best results, make sure the oil in the tin is very hot before adding the batter, and avoid opening the oven door during cooking as it can cause the puddings to collapse.

1   First prepare the Yorkshire pudding batter. Sift the flour into a large bowl and add a pinch of salt and pepper. Whisk the eggs and milk together in a separate bowl, then add to the flour and whisk until you have a smooth batter. Leave to rest.

2   Preheat the oven to 200°C/400°F/gas mark 6.

3   Season the beef with salt and pepper and drizzle with sunflower oil. **(a)**

4   Heat a roasting pan and, when hot, brown the beef on all sides. **(b)** Arrange the carrots, onion and garlic in the roasting pan and sit the meat on the vegetables. **(c)** Roast for 15–20 minutes. Reduce the heat to 160°C/325°F/gas mark 3 and baste the beef with the juices. **(d)** Roast for the following times per 450g (1lb):

Rare: 12–13 minutes

Medium-rare: 17–18 minutes

Well done: 22–24 minutes

5   Meanwhile, place the potatoes in a saucepan, cover with water and bring to the boil. Reduce the heat and simmer for 10 minutes. Strain and give the potatoes a little shake to fluff the edges. Put the fat in a roasting pan and place in the oven until melted. Add the potatoes to the hot fat, place them on the top shelf in the oven and roast for 25–35 minutes. The beef should be moved to the bottom of the oven. Once it is removed from the oven to rest, increase the oven temperature to 190°C/375°F/gas mark 5.

6 About 30 minutes before you are ready to serve, take a 12-hole muffin tin and quarter-fill each hole with sunflower oil. Place in the oven for 5–10 minutes, until the oil is sizzling, then spoon in enough batter to half-fill each hole. Bake for 15–20 minutes on the top shelf, until the puddings are well risen and golden brown.

7 When the beef is done to your liking, transfer it to a meat plate, cover loosely with kitchen foil and leave to rest for 25–30 minutes.

8 Now make the gravy. Place the roasting pan on the hob or stove, add the flour to the remaining juices and stir until the mixture becomes dry and lumpy. **(e)** Slowly add the wine and stock, whisking as you do so. **(f)** Strain through a fine sieve or strainer into a clean saucepan and cook for a further 2–4 minutes. **(g)** Taste and adjust the seasoning if necessary.

9 Carve the beef at the last minute and serve with the Yorkshire puddings, roast potatoes and gravy.

e

f

g

Tips and ideas

- The beef can be served with Béarnaise Sauce (see page 72) if you like.

- Roast whole garlic cloves with the potatoes to add extra flavour.

Striploin Steaks with Pont-neuf Potatoes

Serves 4

2 sprigs of thyme
2 bay leaves
3–4 black peppercorns
85ml (⅓ cup) olive oil
4 striploin steaks, about 200–225g
　(7–8oz) each
Sunflower oil, for deep-frying
4 large potatoes (Maris Piper, russets
　or similar)

For the flavoured butter
100g (1 stick) butter
Zest of ½ lemon
3 garlic cloves, chopped
2 tbsp chopped flat leaf parsley
Salt and black pepper

Tips and ideas

- After brushing your steak with oil, add some rock salt to the pan and, once it starts smoking or popping, immediately add the steak and it will have a beautiful barbecued flavour.

- It's important to let the steaks cook undisturbed for the first minute or two on each side so that the meat seals and colours.

- The steak can be served with thick hand-cut chips (fries) or wedges if you prefer.

- I like to slice the cooked steak along the grain and serve it with my favourite sauce (Béarnaise – see page 72) plus vegetables and creamy mashed potato.

I recommend using a griddle pan for cooking the steaks as it reaches a higher temperature than an ordinary frying pan or grill. Pont-neuf potatoes are thin batons, usually cut about 1cm (½ inch) thick and 8cm (3 inches) long.

1 Place the thyme and bay leaves in a large bowl with the peppercorns, pour in the olive oil and stir thoroughly to combine the flavours. Add the steaks and leave to marinate, preferably in the refrigerator overnight, but for at least 30 minutes. **(a)**

2 To make the flavoured butter, place the butter in a bowl and beat until softened. Add the lemon zest, garlic and parsley and mix thoroughly. Taste and season with salt and pepper if necessary, then roll the butter into a cylinder shape, wrap in clingfilm (plastic wrap) and chill.

3 Preheat sunflower oil in a deep-fat fryer to 160°C/325°F. Alternatively, pour a one-third depth of oil into a deep saucepan and heat to the same temperature.

4 Meanwhile, peel the potatoes and cut into chips (fries) 1cm (½ inch) thick. **(e)** Deep-fry for 3–5 minutes without colouring, then lift them on to kitchen paper (paper towels) and increase the temperature of the oil to 190°C/375°F. **(f)** Return the chips to the oil and deep-fry for a further 4–5 minutes, until crisp and golden. **(g)** Transfer to a plate lined with kitchen paper to drain. **(h)**

5 While the chips are cooking, place a griddle (ridged grill) pan over a medium-high heat. When hot, remove the excess oil from the steaks and season with salt and pepper. **(b)** Then sear as follows **(c)**:

Rare: 2–3 minutes on each side

Medium-rare: 4 minutes on each side

Well done: 5–6 minutes on each side

Transfer the steaks to a plate and leave to rest for at least 3–4 minutes before serving. **(d)**

6 Put the Pont-neuf potatoes on to serving plates and place a steak on each plate. Add a slice of the flavoured butter to each steak and serve straight away.

e

f

g

h

Poultry

Cooking Poultry

Poultry is the general term used for all domestic fowl bred for food. The flesh of poultry is more easily digested than red meats, such as beef and lamb, and contains protein that's important for building tissues and providing energy. The flesh is low in fat, and by removing the skin you can reduce the fat content even further.

The rule when buying any poultry is to go for a free-range bird of the best quality you can afford. It may be more expensive than the usual supermarket offering, but the flavour will be vastly superior.

Chicken: Probably the most popular form of poultry, and endlessly versatile. When buying, look for a bird with plump breasts and firm flesh. Corn-fed chickens have yellow flesh, which tends to be firmer than that of other birds, but generally has more flavour.

Duck: Has a lovely layer of fat directly under the skin that helps to keep the meat moist. Much of it is released when roasted, and it's worth saving to make excellent roast potatoes. We cook the breast lightly so that it is still pink, and use the legs for making confit, which is cooked duck preserved in its own fat in airtight jars. Over a period of time it becomes so tender that, when reheated, the meat literally falls off the bone.

Goose: Used mainly as an alternative to turkey at Christmas-time. Like duck, it has copious amounts of fat that makes wonderful roast potatoes. Goose has a richer flavour than turkey, but can be stuffed and carved in the same way, which makes it perfect for the smaller family.

Guinea fowl: About the size of a small chicken, this bird has a gamier flavour. It can be cooked in the same ways as pheasant and chicken.

Quail: Being small and plump when in season, quail are ideal as a one-person portion. Their flavour is slightly gamy.

Turkey: Usually a Christmas bird, but now available all year round. Try to use the bronze variety because the flavour is worth the extra expense.

How to joint a bird

1   Using a sharp knife, cut through the skin between the leg and breast on both sides of the bird.

2   Insert your thumbs into the joints, grasp the legs and push them away from the body. **(a)** Insert your knife and cut down through the joint to release each leg.

3   With the breastbone pointing towards you, bring the knife in horizontally through the rear cavity until you reach the wing bone, and cut until the back falls away from the crown. **(b)**

4   Turn the bird breast-side up and cut down toward the wing joint to remove the wing. **(c)** Repeat on the other side.

5   Cut along the centre of the breastbone to separate the breasts, then cut each breast in half. **(d)**

6   To separate the drumstick from the thigh, run a sharp knife around the joint, then push the flesh slightly back on to the bone. **(e)**

7   Remove the wing tips, then push the flesh down to expose two bones. Remove the smaller of these. **(f)**

8   At this point you should have 12 pieces, namely: 4 breast pieces, 2 wings, 2 wing bones with breast, 2 thighs and 2 drumsticks. Reserve the carcass for stock.

Chicken Risotto

Serves 4

1.2 litres (5 cups) White Chicken Stock
   (see page 87)
4 tbsp olive oil
65g (5 tbsp) butter
2 shallots, finely chopped
2 sprigs of thyme
450g (2⅓ cups) Carnaroli rice or other
   Aroborio or risotto rice
120ml (½ cup) dry white wine
400g (14oz) boneless, skinless chicken
   thighs, cut into 1cm (½ inch) pieces
75g (3oz) streaky (fatty) bacon, finely
   chopped
200g (3 cups) button mushrooms,
   thinly sliced
Salt and black pepper
120g (1½ cups) Parmesan cheese,
   finely grated, plus extra to serve
   (optional)
50ml (¼ cup) double (heavy) cream
Juice of ½ lemon

a

b

All too often, risotto is gluey and tasteless, but there's no need for that to happen if you follow this recipe. Using good-quality chicken stock is a must.

1   Pour the stock into a large saucepan and bring just to the boil. Reduce the heat and keep it at a gentle simmer.

2   Put 3 tablespoons of the oil and 40g (3 tbsp) of the butter into a wide, heavy-based saucepan over a low heat. When the butter has melted, add the shallots and thyme. Cook very gently for 45–60 seconds, until completely softened.

3   Add the rice and stir well for 1 minute, ensuring it is glazed but does not stick to the bottom of the pan.

4   Pour in the wine and continue slowly stirring the rice until the wine has evaporated.

5   Start adding the chicken stock a ladleful at a time, stirring gently now and then, and allowing each addition to be absorbed before adding the next one. **(a)** It is vitally important not to rush this process. Continue in this way until all the liquid has been absorbed and the rice is plump and tender – about 18–22 minutes. **(b)**

6   Meanwhile, place the remaining oil in a large frying pan over a high heat. When hot, cook the chicken and bacon for 1–2 minutes. Add the mushrooms and cook for a further 2 minutes. Season with salt and pepper.

7   Fold the chicken mixture into the risotto, add the Parmesan and cream and combine gently. Stir in the lemon juice and remaining butter. Season to taste and serve immediately with extra Parmesan cheese, if you like.

Tips and ideas

• Risotto rice consists of plump, medium-to-short grains that contain a high proportion of starch. This is what gives risotto its trademark creaminess. Don't be tempted to use long-grain rice because its starch works in the opposite way, to produce separate grains.

Chilli-salted Chicken Wings

Serves 4

2 tbsp sunflower oil
Zest and juice of 2 limes
4 tbsp soy sauce
2 tbsp honey
1 long red chilli, chopped
2cm (¾ inch) piece of fresh ginger,
  grated
3 garlic cloves, chopped
14–18 chicken wings
2 tsp dried chilli flakes
2–3 tbsp sea salt
1 quantity Marie-Rose Sauce, to serve
  (see page 64)

Everyone loves chicken wings – they're economical and very adaptable. Flavoured with various marinades or seasonings to make them hot and spicy or sweet and tangy, they're irresistible.

1   Combine the oil, lime juice, soy sauce, honey, fresh chilli, ginger and garlic in a large bowl. Add the chicken wings and toss to coat in the mixture. Cover with clingfilm (plastic wrap) and leave to marinate in the refrigerator for 30 minutes.

2   Preheat the oven to 180°C/350°F/gas mark 4.

3   Place the chilli flakes, lime zest and sea salt in a small mortar and crush together with the pestle. Set aside.

4   Arrange the chicken wings in a roasting pan and roast for 30–45 minutes, until cooked through. Give them a shake every so often to keep them covered with the glaze and prevent them from sticking to the tin.

5   Serve the wings sprinkled with the chilli salt and offer the Marie-Rose Sauce for dipping.

Tips and ideas

- Use Guinness, teriyaki sauce, Tomato Sauce (see page 78) or tomato ketchup instead of the soy sauce, and add sweetness with either sugar or honey.

- Wings can be dry-seasoned if you like. Simply dust them with paprika, chilli powder, coriander seed, lemon thyme or rosemary.

- Chicken wings are very economical, and suitable for barbecuing, grilling (broiling) or frying.

Chicken Pâté en Croûte

Serves 10–12

625g (1¼lb) boneless, skinless chicken
  thighs, diced
100g (4oz) pork fat, skinned and cut
  into batons
1 tbsp chopped oregano
1 tbsp chopped flat leaf parsley
50ml (¼ cup) white wine
150ml (⅔ cup) double (heavy) cream
1 egg plus 1 egg yolk
Salt and black pepper
100g (1 stick) butter, plus extra for
  greasing
500g (18oz) boneless, skinless chicken
  breasts, cut into long strips
2 onions, finely chopped
100g (1½ cups) mushrooms, finely
  sliced
2 tbsp rapeseed (canola) oil
400g (14oz) chicken livers
2 quantities Suet Pastry (see page 42)
Plain (all-purpose) flour, for dusting
250g (9oz) streaky (fatty) bacon,
  thinly sliced
1 egg mixed with 1 tbsp milk, for
  brushing

This pâté en croûte is delicious for picnics, brunch or family events. It is best prepared a day or two in advance.

1   Place the chicken thigh meat in a large bowl and add the pork fat and herbs. Pour in the wine, then cover with clingfilm (plastic wrap) and leave to marinate in the refrigerator, preferably overnight, or for at least 3–4 hours. **(a)**

2   Once marinated, place the chicken in a food processor or blender, then add the cream, egg and egg yolk and season with salt and pepper. Pulse once or twice, until the meat is coarsely chopped. **(b)**

3   Melt half the butter in a large frying pan. Add the chicken strips and sauté over a high heat for 1–2 minutes, until caramelized. **(c)** Transfer to a plate and set aside.

4   Add the remaining butter to the pan and reduce the heat. When melted, add the onions and mushrooms and sauté gently for 4–5 minutes, until very soft. Transfer to another plate and set aside.

5   Wipe out the pan and heat the oil in it. Add the chicken livers, season with salt and pepper and cook for 1 minute. **(d)** Transfer to a bowl and set aside.

6   Preheat the oven to 180°C/350°F/gas mark 4. Grease a terrine measuring 32 x 11 x 8cm (13 x 4 x 3 inches).

7   Roll out the dough on a lightly floured work surface and use two-thirds of it to line the terrine. Trim off the excess.

8   Line the pastry case (shell) with the bacon, allowing it to overhang the edges. Spread half the onions and mushrooms in the terrine, season with salt and pepper, then spoon one-third of the marinated chicken mixture on top. Sprinkle with half the chicken livers and chicken strips. Cover with another third of the chicken mixture, then add the remaining chicken strips and livers. Spread the remaining chicken mixture over them, then add the remaining onions and mushrooms. Fold the overhanging bacon over the filling. **(e)**

9   Brush the edge of the pastry with the egg wash and cover with the remaining pastry. Trim off the excess with a knife, then flute the edges by pressing the back of a knife into the pastry at regular intervals. **(f)** Reroll the trimmings and cut out various shapes to decorate the top. Brush the entire surface with more egg wash.

10 Now you have to make a 'chimney' for the steam to escape. Cut a piece of kitchen foil measuring 8 x 8cm (3 x 3 inches) and roll it into a cylinder. Cut a steam hole of the same diameter in the top of the pastry and insert the chimney to prevent the hole closing as the pâté bakes. **(g)**

11 Place the terrine in a roasting pan and pour enough boiling water around it to come about one-quarter of the way up the sides. Bake for 20–25 minutes, then reduce the heat to 160°C/325°F/gas mark 3 and bake for a further 40 minutes. Leave to cool, then invert the terrine on to a plate. Refrigerate until required. Serve with a crisp fresh salad and chutney.

e

f

Tips and ideas

- The suet pastry releases steam while baking, so the chimney is needed to allow it to escape.

- To help hold the terrine together, it's common to pour a jelly (gelatin) into the chimney about 10 minutes before the pâté is cooked through. Simply soak 2–3 gelatine leaves or sheets in cold water for 15 minutes. When soft, squeeze dry and place in a saucepan with 100ml (½ cup) port and 100ml (½ cup) chicken stock or red wine and heat until combined.

- To help ensure even baking and reduce the chance of undercooking the pastry, this pâté en croûte is best made in a rectangular mould, though an oval-shaped one could be used instead.

- Add nuts or dry fruit to the mixture to add crunch to the pâté.

- The basic pâté may be cooked alone, then stored in sterilized jars (see tip, page 78) as a preserve. Refrigerate in hot regions.

g

Chicken and Broccoli Stir-fry

Serves 4

2 tbsp sunflower oil
2 boneless, skinless chicken breasts,
   about 150g/5oz each, cut into
   thin strips
Salt and black pepper
1 head of broccoli, cut into florets
1 red onion, thinly sliced
2 garlic cloves, finely chopped
½ green chilli, thinly chopped
4 tbsp oyster sauce
100ml (½ cup) water

Stir-fries are probably the most flexible meals you can make because virtually anything can go into them. My favourite meat for them is chicken, and it is important to get the oil smoking hot before you start cooking.

1   Prepare all the ingredients and place them by the side of your hob or stove.

2   Place a wok or large frying pan over a high heat and add half the oil. When hot, add half the chicken, season with salt and pepper and stir-fry for 2–3 minutes, until brown and cooked through. **(a)** Transfer to a warm plate. Cook the remaining chicken in the same way and add to the plate.

3   Add the remaining oil to the pan. When hot, stir-fry the broccoli, onion, garlic and chilli for 1 minute. **(b)**

4   Return the cooked chicken to the pan and pour in the oyster sauce and water. Cover with a lid and cook for 2 minutes, until the vegetables are just tender.

5   Taste and adjust the seasoning if necessary, then serve immediately on a bed of boiled rice or fried rice.

Tips and ideas

- When stir-frying, wait a second before tossing to allow the meat to brown and caramelize.

- Try to cut all the meat and vegetables into bite-sized pieces so they will all cook quickly in the same amount of time.

- Oyster sauce can be rather salty, so taste both the sauce and the chicken before adding.

- To make fluffy boiled rice, measure the uncooked rice in a jug or cup and add it to 3 times that volume of boiling salted water. Simmer for 12–15 minutes, then drain and serve immediately.

- The best oils for stir-frying are peanut, vegetable and rapeseed (canola) oil.

- For a final flourish, you can garnish the finished dish with a drizzle of sesame oil and a sprinkling of sesame seeds.

a

b

Chicken Ballotines with Smoked Cheese Gnocchi in Herb Butter

Serves 4

2 boneless, skinless chicken breasts,
  about 150g (5oz) each, diced
100g (½ cup) ricotta or cream cheese
1 egg white
5 garlic cloves, lightly crushed
2 tbsp chopped chives
Salt and black pepper
4 large boneless chicken thighs, about
  100–120g (3½–4½oz) each
500 ml (2 cups) Brown Chicken Stock
  (see page 86)
2 sprigs of thyme
75g (6 tbsp) butter, cubed
3 tbsp olive oil

For the gnocchi
325g (11½oz) Rooster, russets or other
  floury potatoes (about 2), unpeeled
  and pricked with a fork
2 tbsp salt
50g (½ cup) smoked cheese, grated
1 egg yolk
50g (⅓ cup) plain (all-purpose) flour
Rice flour, semolina flour or plain flour,
  for dusting

A ballotine is a poached parcel or package of meat, usually made with chicken or duck stuffed with a juicy filling, then fried to crisp it up. The gnocchi make an elegant accompaniment to the ballotine, and are also a delicious vegetarian option on their own.

1   Preheat the oven to 180°C/350°F/gas mark 4.

2   Place the chicken breasts in a blender or food processor and pulse until smooth. Add the ricotta, egg white, 3 of the garlic cloves, the chives and season with salt and pepper, then pulse again to combine. Transfer the mixture to a piping (pastry) bag fitted with a 1cm (½ inch) nozzle (tip) and chill for 1 hour, until firm. **(a)**

3   Meanwhile, prepare the gnocchi. Place the potatoes on a bed of rock salt in a roasting pan and bake for 30 minutes, until softened. Leave to cool for 5 minutes, then peel.

4   Pass the potato flesh through a ricer, or mash thoroughly in a large bowl. Beat in the smoked cheese and egg yolk, then season well. Mix in the plain flour – just enough to ensure the dough is not too sticky for rolling.

5   Divide the dough into 3 equal pieces and roll into long cylinder shapes about 2cm (¾ inch) in diameter. (Dust the work surface with a little rice flour if you find the dough sticky to roll.) Using a sharp knife, cut the dough into pieces about 2cm (¾ inch) long. Roll each of them into an oblong shape, place on a plate or tray and chill for a few minutes.

6   Place each chicken thigh between two sheets of clingfilm (plastic wrap) and flatten with a rolling pin or heavy-based saucepan to an even thickness of about 5mm (¼ inch). **(b)** Spread out a large sheet of clingfilm and place a flattened chicken thigh in the middle of it, skin-side down. Season with salt and pepper, then pipe one- quarter of the chicken mousse at one end of the meat. **(c)** Using the clingfilm to help, roll the chicken up tightly around the filling to create a cylinder shape. **(d)** Remove the clingfilm, then tie string around the middle and both ends of the rolled chicken. **(e)** Repeat this process with the remaining thighs.

7   Place the stock, remaining garlic cloves and the thyme in a medium saucepan and bring to the boil. Add the chicken parcels, cover with a lid and leave to poach, off the heat, for about 20 minutes. **(f)**

8   Using a slotted spoon, remove the parcels from the pan and drain on kitchen paper (paper towels). Leave to cool slightly, then pat dry again.

9   Return the stock to the boil and boil rapidly until it has reduced to a syrupy consistency. Remove the thyme and garlic, then whisk in 25g (2 tbsp) of the butter, off the heat, until well combined.

10 Just before serving, put the oil and remaining butter in a large nonstick frying pan and place over a medium-low heat. When the butter has melted, add the chicken parcels and the gnocchi and fry for 3–5 minutes, until the outside of both is crisp and golden. Season well.

11 Place the chicken and gnocchi on warm serving plates and spoon over the reduced sauce to serve.

Tips and ideas

- Gnocchi can be made in advance and stored for 2 days in the refrigerator, or 2 months in the freezer.

- To test that the gnocchi mixture is the right consistency, drop a piece of it into boiling water: if it breaks up, you need to add a little more flour.

- To serve these gnocchi as a vegetarian main course, sauté them in mushroom and herb butter.

- To give the ballotines a neater appearance, they can be rolled up in clingfilm for poaching. It's important to wind the film around at least twice and tie a firm knot at both ends.

Coq au Vin

Serves 4

50g (4 tbsp) butter
2 tbsp olive oil
1 whole chicken, about 1.6kg (3½lb)
   divided into 12 pieces (see page 116)
Salt and black pepper
100g (4oz) streaky (fatty) bacon, cut
   into small strips
300g (4 cups) button mushrooms,
   quartered or sliced
20 baby (pearl) onions, peeled
   but left whole
3 garlic gloves, crushed
1 tsp tomato purée (paste)
600ml (2½ cups) red wine
200ml (1 cup) Brown Chicken Stock
   (see page 86)
3-4 sprigs of thyme
2 bay leaves
Beurre manié, to thicken (see tip
   below)
Chopped flat leaf parsley, to garnish

Tips and ideas

- To make beurre manié, combine
  35g (¼ cup) plain (all-purpose) flour
  with 35g (2½ tbsp) softened butter
  until it forms a thick paste. **(f)** Whisk
  into sauces or soups near the end
  of the cooking process.

- Using white wine instead of red
  wine will produce a lighter version
  of the dish.

This is a classic French dish, usually made with a cockerel. If you can find one, let it cook for 20–30 minutes longer than specified below because the meat is slightly tougher than ordinary chicken. I like to use a whole bird that I joint myself, but drumsticks and thighs can be used if preferred.

1   Preheat the oven to 180°C/350°F/gas mark 4.

2   Place the butter and oil in a large frying pan over a medium heat. When hot, fry the chicken pieces for 2-3 minutes, until golden brown all over. **(a)** Season well, then transfer to a casserole dish.

3   Add the bacon to the empty pan and fry for 2 minutes, or until browned. Transfer to the casserole dish. **(b)**

4   Add the mushrooms, onions and garlic to the empty pan and cook for 4-5 minutes, until glazed and golden brown. **(c)** Stir in the tomato purée, wine and stock, bring to the boil, then pour over the chicken in the casserole dish. **(d)** Add the thyme and bay leaves, then cover and bake for 40-45 minutes, until the chicken is cooked through. **(e)**

5   Using a slotted spoon, transfer the chicken pieces to a plate, cover with kitchen foil and keep warm.

6   Remove the thyme and bay leaves from the sauce, then bring it back to the boil. Add small pieces of the beurre manié to the boiling liquid (it is very important that the liquid is boiling or the sauce will be lumpy) and whisk rapidly until the sauce thickens. **(g)** Taste and adjust the seasoning if necessary.

7   Return the chicken pieces to the casserole dish, stir gently to coat in the sauce and garnish with the parsley. **(h)** Serve with mashed potatoes.

e

f

g

h

Poached Chicken Noodle Salad

Serves 4

750ml (3 cups) White Chicken Stock
  (see page 87)
3 sprigs of thyme
2 sprigs of oregano
Salt and black pepper
2 boneless, skinless chicken breasts,
  about 150g (5oz) each
400g (14oz) rice noodles
1 tbsp sesame oil
1 red (bell) pepper, deseeded and
  thinly sliced
1 red onion, thinly sliced
3 radishes, thinly sliced
2.5cm (1 inch) piece of fresh ginger,
  chopped
100ml (½ cup) soy sauce
50g (2 cups) fresh coriander (cilantro),
  chopped

Here's a great recipe for a light lunch or quick supper. It has just a hint of ginger to spice it up.

1   Place the chicken stock and herbs in a saucepan over a medium heat, season with salt and pepper and bring to the boil.

2   Reduce the stock to a simmer, add the chicken, then cover and poach for 12–14 minutes. Remove from the heat and leave the chicken in the stock for a further 8–10 minutes, until cooked through and infused with the flavoured stock.

3   Transfer the herbs and chicken to a plate, cover with kitchen foil and keep warm.

4   Place the pan of stock back over the heat and bring to the boil. Add the noodles and cook according to the packet instructions. Strain, then drizzle with the sesame oil.

5   Shred the chicken and add to the noodles, along with the red pepper, onion, radishes, ginger and soy sauce. Use your hands to combine everything, then sprinkle with the coriander. Serve immediately.

Tips and ideas

- Poaching is a very gentle way of cooking, and using good stock imparts extra flavour. Chicken cooked this way can be used for all sorts of things, from quiches and simple pasta dishes to sandwich fillings.

- Use egg noodles instead of rice noodles, or try quinoa.

Fish

Cooking Fish

You might ask why would you fillet a fish yourself when you can easily buy fillets from a fishmonger or supermarket. The answer is quality. To be certain of buying the best, you need to look at the whole fish. The eyes should be bright and clear, the flesh firm, and there should be no unpleasant odour. Truly fresh fish should smell of the sea.

Another reason I like to fillet my own fish is so that I can use the bones and trimmings to make stock. The best are those from flat fish, because they are higher in gelatine and make a better stock.

The fish that I fillet are either flat fish, such as plaice, sole, turbot, brill and halibut, or round fish, such as mackerel, trout, cod, salmon, sea bass and monkfish.

How to scale, skin and fillet fish

It is important to have the right tool for the job – in this case, a knife with a sharp, flexible blade. Kitchen scissors are handy too.

Flat fish

1   Rinse the fish under cold running water and pat dry with kitchen paper (paper towels).

2   Using kitchen scissors, cut away the fins as close to the flesh as possible. **(a)**

3   With a sharp knife, cut across the tail of the fish.

4   Cut around the back of the head down to the backbone. **(b)**

5   Cut along the centre of the fish from head to tail. **(c)**

6   Starting at the head end, slide the blade under the flesh, as close to the bone as possible. Move the knife back and forth along the bone to slice off the fillet and repeat this step on the other side to remove the 2 top fillets. **(d)** Turn the fish over and repeat this step on the other side. **(e/f)** At this point you should have 4 fish fillets.

7   Push the tip of the knife under the skin at the narrowest end of each fillet to create a small flap. Holding the fish flesh-side down with one hand, lift the flap of skin with the other hand and pull off the whole skin in one sweeping motion.

Round fish

1 Rinse the fish under cold running water and pat dry with kitchen paper (paper towels).

2 Grip the fish by its tail and, using either a fish-scaler or blunt knife, scrape off the scales. **(a)** Rinse under cold running water.

3 Lay the fish on a clean chopping (cutting) board and, starting at the head end, cut diagonally just behind the gills on both sides of the body to remove the head. **(b)**

4 Starting from the head end, cut through the flesh to one side of the backbone, using gentle sweeping motions along the whole length of fish. **(c/d)** Try to keep as close to the bone as possible. Turn the fish over and repeat this step. At this point you should have 2 fish fillets.

5 Using kitchen scissors, snip off the fins. Then, holding the fish flesh-side down with one hand and lifting the skin with the other, pull off the skin in one sweeping movement.

How to remove fish bones after cooking

The technique for boning fish after it has been cooked depends on the shape.

Cooked whole flat fish

1   Place the fish on a plate, then remove the lateral bones with a fork or spoon.

2   Run a sharp knife along the centre of the fish. Slide the blade underneath the flesh and gently ease the fillet away from the bone. **(a)** Repeat with the opposite fillet.

3   Grasp the tail and lift it up, taking all the bones with it. **(b)** Remove any stray bones with your fingers or tweezers.

4   Transfer the fish to warmed plates for serving.

Cooked whole round fish

1   Place the fish on a plate. Insert a fork under the skin and lift it off.

2   Using a spoon and/or fork, slide the flesh off the bones in a sweeping manner. This gives you one boneless fillet.

3   To release the second fillet, grasp the tail and lift it up, taking all the bones with it. Remove any stray bones with your fingers or tweezers.

4   Transfer the fish to warmed plates for serving.

Bouillabaisse and Rouille Sauce

Serves 6

1kg (2¼lb) baby new potatoes
3 pinches of saffron
1kg (2¼lb) John Dory, monkfish, sea
  bass or sea bream, cut into bite-sized
  chunks
300g (11oz) mussels, scrubbed
18 raw Dublin Bay prawns
  (langoustines), deveined (see tip,
  page 146)
Samphire, to serve

For the rouille
1 potato, about 90g (3½oz)
3 pinches of saffron
2 tbsp boiling water
2 egg yolks
2 garlic cloves, crushed
Sea salt and black pepper
250ml (1 cup) extra virgin olive oil

For the stock
4 tbsp olive oil
1 large leek, white parts only, sliced
2 onions, roughly chopped
2 garlic cloves, crushed
2 fennel bulbs, fronds reserved
8 ripe tomatoes, roughly chopped
1 tsp tomato purée (paste)
1 large bouquet garni
3 stems each of oregano, chervil and
  parsley
1kg (2¼lb) fish bones (e.g. John Dory,
  turbot, monkfish)
4 tsp Pernod
1 quantity Fish Stock (see page 86)
3 pinches of saffron

This is my version of a traditional French fish soup that I learnt while working on cruise ships. Steamed samphire, a type of sea vegetable, makes a lovely accompaniment. The garlicky rouille is a wonderful garnish for any fish or fish soup, and I love it simply spread on good bread. The flavour of the stock improves if left overnight, so you could prepare it a day before you want to poach the fish.

1   First prepare the rouille. Wash the potato, then place it in a saucepan and cover with cold water. Bring to the boil and simmer for about 30 minutes.

2   Meanwhile, crush the saffron strands in a small bowl. Add 2 tablespoons boiling water and leave to soak. **(a)**

3   Peel the potato and mash it to a smooth purée. Leave to cool slightly.

4   Put the potato and egg yolks into a bowl with the garlic, saffron mixture and salt and pepper and mix well. **(b)** Pour in the olive oil very slowly, beating constantly with a wooden spoon, as if making mayonnaise, until you have a thick, glossy sauce. **(c)** Taste and adjust the seasoning if necessary. Cover with clingfilm (plastic wrap) and refrigerate until required. (It will keep fairly well for 2–3 days.)

5   To prepare the stock, heat the oil in a large saucepan, add the leek, onions, garlic and fennel and cook for 2 minutes, until softened. **(d)** Add the tomatoes, tomato purée, bouquet garni, herb stems and fish bones. Pour in the Pernod, then carefully flambé to burn off the alcohol. **(e)** When the flames have died down, add the fish stock and saffron, bring to the boil, then reduce the heat and simmer for 20–25 minutes.

6   Meanwhile, place the baby potatoes in a large saucepan of salted water and add the saffron. Bring to the boil and simmer for 15 minutes, until slightly firm. Drain and cut each potato in half. **(f)** Set aside.

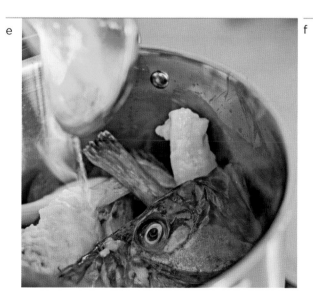

g

h

i

j

7 Strain the fish stock in a large sieve or strainer, rubbing it through with the back of a ladle. **(g)** Discard all the solids. Strain the stock twice more, this time through a fine sieve, again rubbing it with a ladle. Taste and adjust the seasoning if necessary.

8 To assemble the bouillabaisse, place the potatoes in a large saucepan and pour the stock over them. Bring to the boil, then simmer for 5 minutes.

9 Add the fish chunks and mussels, and simmer for a further 5–8 minutes. **(h/i)** Add the prawns 2–3 minutes before serving, or when the fish is just firm, the potatoes are soft, the prawns are tender and all the mussels have opened (discard any that remain closed. **(j)** Serve with samphire and the rouille, offered separately.

Tips and ideas for rouille

- The potato should still be warm when you crush it. Add the oil little by little so that the potato retains its creamy texture.

- Breadcrumbs soaked in warm milk can be used instead of potato.

- Add a dash of lemon juice to the rouille if you like.

- If your garlic is very strongly flavoured, blanch it in boiling water for 30–40 seconds before crushing.

- Try to use a mild extra virgin olive oil in the rouille. If what you have is too strong, mix it with a little sunflower oil.

Tips and ideas for bouillabaisse

- To devein a prawn, using a small, sharp knife, make a very shallow cut all the way down the back of the prawn and remove the black line.

- Croûtons add crunch to the soup and make a good contrast to the other ingredients.

- If you'd like a spicy bouillabaisse, add a few pinches of chilli powder to the stock.

- To turn the bouillabaisse into a seafood chowder, add 200ml (1 cup) double (heavy) cream to the final mixture.

- If you don't have any saffron, try turmeric instead. It's not the same, but is a satisfactory replacement.

Fish Goujons with Chunky Chips

Serves 4

4 large potatoes, Maris Piper, russets
  or Golden Wonder
Sunflower oil, for deep-frying
Plain (all-purpose) flour, for dusting
4 cod fillets, about 150g (5oz) each,
  sliced into goujons (finger-width
  strips)
4 wedges of lemon (optional)

For the batter

200g (1⅔ cups) plain flour
75g (⅔ cup) cornflour (cornstarch)
250ml (1 cup) lager, freshly opened
100ml (½ cup) soda water (club soda)

For the tartare sauce

250g (1¼ cups) Mayonnaise (see
  page 64)
2 tbsp gherkins (or pickles), chopped
1 tbsp capers, chopped
2 shallots, finely diced
Juice of 1 lemon
½ tsp horseradish sauce (optional)

For the pea purée

20g (1½ tbsp) butter
½ onion
2 garlic cloves
150ml (⅔ cup) double (heavy) cream
50ml (¼ cup) white wine
225g (1½ cups) fresh peas, podded
Salt and black pepper
1 tbsp chopped mint

Tips and ideas

- When adding the battered fish to
  the oil, lower it in gradually, gently
  sweeping it back and forth. This will
  prevent the batter sticking to the
  frying basket.

Nothing beats the crunch of deep-fried battered fish strips. The crispy batter is a great contrast to the soft, flaky fish.

1 First make the batter. Sift the flour and cornflour into a bowl. **(a)** Make a well in the centre and gradually whisk in the lager and soda water until you have a smooth batter. **(b/c)** Cover with clingfilm (plastic wrap) and leave to rest at room temperature for at least 30–40 minutes. **(d)**

2 Meanwhile, make the tartare sauce. Place all the ingredients for it in a bowl, mix well, cover with clingfilm (plastic wrap) and store in the refrigerator until required.

3 Peel the potatoes and cut into thick chips (fries). Place in a bowl of water until you're ready to cook them.

4 To make the pea purée, melt the butter in a saucepan over a medium heat. Add the onion and garlic and fry for 1 minute, until softened. Pour in the cream and wine and bring to the boil. Add the peas and simmer for 3–4 minutes, until they have softened. Remove from the heat, season with salt and pepper and stir in the mint.

5 Transfer the pea mixture to a blender or food processor and blend so that it is still a little chunky. Keep warm.

6 Preheat sunflower oil in a deep-fat fryer to 180°C/350°F. Alternatively, pour a one-third depth of oil into a deep saucepan and heat until a cube of bread browns in 1 minute.

7 Drain the chips in a colander and pat dry to remove any excess water. Add them in batches to the hot oil and fry for 3–5 minutes, until crisp and fully cooked. Transfer to a bowl lined with kitchen paper (paper towels) and season with salt straight away. Keep hot.

8 Meanwhile, place some flour in a shallow dish and lightly dust the fish strips in it. **(e)** Shake off any excess, then dredge in the batter. **(f)**

9 When the chips are all cooked, deep-fry the fish goujons for about 3–5 minutes, until cooked through and golden brown. **(g)** Transfer the fried fish to a bowl lined with kitchen paper. **(h)** Keep hot.

10 Serve the fish and chips with lemon wedges, if liked, offering the pea purée and tartare sauce separately.

e

f

g

h

Haddock with Walnut and Herb Crust

Serves 6

3 tbsp walnut oil
2 shallots, chopped
1 garlic clove, chopped
75g (1½ cups) fresh white
   breadcrumbs
50g (½ cup) walnuts, toasted
1 tbsp chopped flat leaf parsley
Zest of 1 lemon
Salt and black pepper
6 haddock or halibut fillets, about
   150g (5oz) each

Fish and nuts make a classic combination. Here the walnuts add a lovely crunchy texture to the crust.

1   Preheat the oven to 180°C/350°F/gas mark 4. Line a baking sheet with nonstick baking (parchment) paper.

2   Place half the oil in a frying pan over a low heat. When hot, add the shallots and garlic and cook for 2–3 minutes, until slightly translucent. Remove from the heat and add the breadcrumbs, walnuts, parsley, lemon zest, salt and pepper. Stir with a wooden spoon. If you find the mixture a little dry, add some extra oil.

3   Holding a fish fillet flesh-side up in one hand, spoon the breadcrumb mixture over it and press firmly on to the flesh. **(a)** Transfer to the prepared baking sheet and season with salt and pepper. Repeat this process with all the fillets. **(b)**

4   Bake for 12–15 minutes, until the flesh flakes apart when squeezed between your fingers. Serve immediately with some salad leaves.

a

b

Tips and ideas

- If making this for someone with a nut allergy, use porridge (rolled) oats instead of walnuts, and olive oil instead of walnut oil.

Smoked Salmon Mousse

Serves 4

550g (1¼lb) smoked salmon, sliced
50g (4 tbsp) softened butter
1½ gelatine leaves or sheets
100ml (½ cup) Fish Stock (see page 86)
¼ tsp Worcestershire sauce
Dash of Tabasco sauce
150ml (⅔ cup) double (heavy) cream

To serve
Young salad leaves (greens)
2 tsp olive oil, plus extra for drizzling
Juice of ½ lemon, plus extra for drizzling

Once fresh salmon has been cured, it can be hot-smoked or cold-smoked. Both methods are good, but at Dunbrody we like to cold-smoke wild or organic salmon because we think it gives a better flavour.

1   Place 200g (7oz) of the smoked salmon in a blender or food processor. Add the butter and blend until smooth.

2   Put the gelatine in a small bowl, cover with cold water and leave to soak for 5 minutes, or until soft.

3   Place the stock in a small saucepan over a low heat until lukewarm (45–50°C/113–122°F). Squeeze the gelatine dry and add to the stock, stirring to dissolve. Leave to cool slightly.

4   Add the stock to the smoked salmon mixture in the blender or processor, along with the Worcestershire sauce and Tabasco. Blend again until well combined. Add the cream and blend once more.

5   Line four 150ml (⅔ cup) ramekins with clingfilm (plastic wrap), allowing it to generously overhang the edges. Then use the remaining salmon slices to line the ramekins, allowing it to overhang the edges. Fill each ramekin with mousse and fold the overhanging salmon over it. **(a)** Fold the overhanging clingfilm over the salmon and chill for 2 hours. **(b)**

6   When ready to serve, place the salad leaves in a bowl with the olive oil and lemon juice. Season with salt and pepper and toss gently.

7   Gently unmould each mousse on to a serving plate and top with a little of the salad. Drizzle with extra olive oil and lemon juice and serve straight away.

a

b

Tips and ideas

• Smoked salmon is already salty, so the mousse does not need any extra salt.

• The mousse can be prepared in one large terrine if you like.

Lemon Sole with Beurre Noisette

Serves 4

50g (⅓ cup) plain (all-purpose) flour
Salt and black pepper
4 lemon sole, about 225g (8oz) each,
 cleaned, gutted and skinned
100g (1 stick) butter
2 tbsp sunflower oil
Zest and juice of 1 lemon
2 tbsp capers, rinsed
2 tbsp finely chopped flat leaf parsley

Lemon sole is actually a type of plaice rather than sole. It is best eaten on the bone.

1 Place the flour in a shallow dish and season with salt and pepper. One by one, coat the lemon sole in the flour, patting gently to remove any excess. **(a)**

2 Place half the butter and half the oil in a large nonstick frying pan over a medium heat. When hot, fry the lemon sole two at a time for 3–5 minutes on each side. The flesh should be golden and slightly coming off the bone. **(b)** Transfer the fish to a warmed plate, cover with kitchen foil and keep warm. Add the remaining oil to the pan and fry the remaining fish in the same way. Keep warm as before.

3 Return the empty pan to the heat, add the remaining butter and leave until golden brown. Remove from the heat and add the lemon zest, juice and capers. Taste and adjust the seasoning if necessary.

4 Add the parsley to the sauce, then pour it over the lemon sole and serve immediately.

a

b

Tips and ideas

• Beurre noisette is made from butter that is cooked in a pan until it goes brown and develops a beautiful nutty flavour.

• Try adding some chopped chervil to the beurre noisette to make a delicious sauce.

• Instead of lemon sole you could use black sole, plaice, flounder or turbot.

Salmon en Papillote with Red Pepper Jelly and Summer Vegetables

Serves 4

1 red (bell) pepper, deseeded and
    thinly sliced
1 red onion, thinly sliced
1 baby fennel, cut lengthways into
    4 slices
8 baby carrots, halved, or 1 carrot,
    thinly sliced
4 salmon steaks, about 150g (5oz)
    each
Salt and black pepper
Zest of 2 limes
50g (2 cups) fresh coriander (cilantro),
    chopped
4 tsp olive oil
4 tbsp white wine

**For the red pepper jelly (makes
350ml/1½ cups)**
1 red (bell) pepper, seeded and roughly
    chopped
165g (⅔ cup) caster (superfine) sugar
50ml (¼ cup) white vinegar
2g pectin powder mixed with 1 tbsp
    caster sugar (see tip, page 160)

Cooking food en papillote (in a paper parcel or package) requires very little oil and allows the contents to gently steam, so it's a pretty healthy way to cook. As vegetables are included, it could be argued that this is the equivalent of a 'one-pot' dish.

Red pepper jelly (gelatin) is a wonderful condiment to have in your refrigerator as it goes well with most fish dishes. Unlike many preserves, it does not need to mature. Once set, it can be eaten straight away.

1   Start by making the jelly. Place the red pepper, caster sugar and vinegar in a blender or food processor and blend until smooth. Transfer the mixture to a large stainless steel saucepan and bring to the boil. Stir constantly and boil for 2 minutes. Leave to stand for 10 minutes. This allows the peppers to cook slowly in the residual heat and prevents them floating to the surface.

2   Return the pan to the heat and bring to the boil again. Sprinkle the pectin/sugar mixture into the pan and stir together. Simmer over a medium heat for 2–3 minutes, stirring occasionally. Leave to cool slightly.

3   Pot the jelly into screwtop sterilized jars (see tip, page 78). Label and date, then store in a cool, dark place for up to 5 months (prepared in a water bath in hot regions). Once opened, store in the refrigerator and use within a month.

4   Preheat the oven to 190°C/375°F/gas mark 5.

5   Cut four sheets of nonstick baking (parchment) paper to 42 x 30 cm (16 x 12 inches). Fold each sheet in half widthways and neatly arrange a pile of the red pepper, onion, fennel and carrots in the centre of them. **(a)**

6   Place a salmon steak on each pile of veg and season with salt and pepper. **(b)**

7   Spread 1 tablespoon of red pepper jelly on top of each piece of salmon. **(c)** Add a little lime zest and sprinkle with the coriander. Drizzle 1 teaspoon of olive oil and 1 tablespoon of white wine over each.

8   Bring up the long sides of the parchment over the fish, fold a few times to seal, then twist the ends, rather like a Christmas cracker or candy wrapper. Place the parcels in a roasting pan and bake for 20 minutes. **(d)** Serve immediately, allowing each person to open up their own little parcel.

Tips and ideas

- Pectin is a natural setting agent extracted from citrus peel and apple pomace (the pulp left after pressing). It is used mainly in jams, jellies and chutneys. I do not recommend replacing pectin with gelatine or vice versa. In some areas brands of pectin vary, so check packaging directions for instructions.

- Jam sugar is available in some supermarkets, which can be used instead of the pectin/caster sugar mixture.

- Add herb pesto instead of red pepper jelly.

- Enclosing the fish in foil and then nonstick baking paper prevents the paper going soggy, and can make it easier to transfer the parcels from the roasting pan to the plates.

- Any fish can be used in this dish – sea bass, turbot, monkfish, cod, etc. For portions smaller than specified above, reduce the cooking time by 2 minutes to ensure the fish stays moist.

- Whole fish can also be cooked en papillote, but in this case I advise using just kitchen foil for the wrapping. A whole salmon of 1.5kg (3¼lb) will take 35–40 minutes in an oven preheated to 190°C/375°F/gas mark 5.

- To make a semicircular parcel, as you see in restaurants, fold one long side of the parchment over the fish so that the paper edges meet. Starting from the folded side, lift up one corner and fold it towards the filling in a small triangle. Keep folding up triangles every 3–5cm (1½–2 inches) right around the parcel until it looks like a semicircle. Tuck the final corner under the parcel to keep the steam inside.

Seafood Gratin with Parmesan and Herb Crumble

Serves 4

300ml (1¼ cups) milk
1 onion, studded with 2 cloves
8 peppercorns
1 bay leaf
25g (2 tbsp) butter
1 onion, thinly sliced
50g (½ cup) button mushrooms
Salt and black pepper
25g (3 tbsp) plain (all-purpose) flour
550g (1¼lb) cod fillet, cut into thin
   strips
100g (4oz) raw prawns (shrimp),
   peeled
Juice of 1 lemon
75g (1⅔ cups) breadcrumbs
25g (¼ cup) Parmesan cheese, grated
1 tbsp chopped parsley
1 tsp chopped dill

I use Parmesan cheese in this crumble because I love the flavour it adds to the dish. For a change of pace, try using a mixture of smoked and white fish.

1   Preheat the oven to 180°C/350°F/gas mark 4.

2   Put the milk in a saucepan with the clove-studded onion, peppercorns and bay leaf and bring to the boil. Remove from the heat, cover with a lid and leave to infuse.

3   Melt the butter in a small saucepan over a medium heat. Add the sliced onion and mushrooms and season with salt and pepper. Cook for 2 minutes, until softened but not browned.

4   Stir in the flour to create a roux and cook for 1 minute. Strain the infused milk and slowly add to the roux, whisking constantly until the sauce is thick and smooth. Bring to the boil, then simmer for a further 2–3 minutes.

5   Place the fish strips and prawns in the bottom of a 25 x 18cm (10 x 7 inch) baking dish. Drizzle with the lemon juice and pour the sauce over the fish.

6   Put the breadcrumbs, Parmesan and herbs into a bowl and mix together using your hands. Season with a little salt and pepper, then sprinkle the breadcrumb mixture all over the sauce.

7   Bake for 25–30 minutes, until the top is golden brown.

8   Serve immediately with some creamy mashed potatoes and green beans.

Tips and ideas

- Top the saucy fish with mashed potato and grated cheese instead of the crumble if you like.

- Add some seasonal vegetables to the dish, such as sweetcorn, fennel, leeks, carrots or cherry tomatoes, depending on the time of year.

- For extra flavour in the sauce, add 1 tsp tomato purée (paste).

Baking and Desserts

Baking Bread

At Dunbrody we still make our breads by hand. These include white, wholemeal (wheat) and sourdough, plus gluten-free bread for coeliac guests.

Types of flour

There are many different types of flours available, and it's important to understand your ingredients before you proceed.

White flour: Strong white flour, sometimes known as bread flour, should be used when bread-making because it has a high gluten content. This makes it stretchy and gives a better rise. Use plain (all-purpose) white flour or self-raising (self-rising) when baking yeast-free breads.

Wholemeal (whole wheat) flour: Milled from the whole wheat kernel, this flour contains lots of bran and wheatgerm, giving it a coarser texture than white flour and making it more nutritious.

Granary (multigrain) flour: Made from a mixture of rye, wholemeal and white flour, granary flour has a lovely nutty, sweet flavour. (Multigrain flour may have up to nine grains.)

Gluten-free flour: Made specially for those who cannot digest the gluten in ordinary flour. Gluten-free flour tends to make smaller, denser loaves than other types of flour, so it's necessary to use slightly more yeast to give the finished bread a more open texture. There's a good variety of gluten-free flours available now in health-food stores and supermarkets. Millet, rye and spelt flour are considered low-gluten flours.

Yeast

Available in several forms, including fresh, dried or fast-acting, yeast is a living organism that is added to bread dough to make it rise. It works through a fermentation process, feeding on the sugar and starches in the flour to produce carbon dioxide, which expands the dough and creates a lighter texture.

White Soda Bread with Sultanas

Makes a 900g (2lb) loaf

450g (3⅔ cups) plain (all-purpose)
  flour, plus extra for dusting
1 rounded tsp bicarbonate of (baking)
  soda
1 tsp salt
75g (½ cup) sultanas (golden raisins)
350ml (1½ cups) buttermilk
2 tbsp milk, for brushing

This is a really nice recipe for traditional
white soda bread. It stays fresh for 3–4 days
in the bread bin, but also freezes successfully.

1   Preheat the oven to 160°C/325°F/gas mark 3. Dust
    a baking sheet with flour.

2   Sift the flour and bicarbonate of soda into a large bowl.
    Add the salt and sultanas and stir to combine.

3   Pour in the buttermilk and mix until a soft and sticky
    dough forms. **(a)**

4   Put the dough on a well-floured work surface and knead
    for a minute or two. **(b)** Shape into a flattened ball and
    place on the prepared baking sheet.

5   Brush the loaf lightly with milk and bake for 45–55 minutes,
    or until the underside sounds hollow when tapped.
    Transfer to a wire rack to cool.

a

b

Tips and ideas

Add any of the following during step 4:

• 2 tbsp chopped nuts, such as hazelnuts, pecans, pine nuts
  or walnuts.

• 2 tbsp poppy, pumpkin, sesame or sunflower seeds.

• 50g (½ cup) grated Cheddar cheese.

• 1 tbsp tomato purée (paste) or mild curry paste.

• 2 tbsp of your favourite herb, such as rosemary or thyme.

Gluten-free Bread

Makes two 425g (15oz) loaves

Sunflower oil, for greasing
450g (3½ cups) good-quality gluten-free flour
2 tsp salt
1 tsp xanthan gum (see tip, page 28)
1 tsp citric acid
20g (2 tbsp plus ¾ tsp) easy-blend dried (active dry) yeast
300–350ml (1¼–1½ cups) water

Here's a great alternative to traditional white soda bread. It stays fresh for 3–4 days in the bread bin, but also freezes well.

1   Grease two 450g (8½ x 4½ x 2½ inch) loaf tins.

2   Sift the flour into a large bowl. (Sifting is essential so that the flour doesn't clump together.) Stir in the salt, xanthan gum, citric acid and dried yeast, then pour in the water and mix until a soft, sticky dough forms.

3   Cut the dough in half and place in the prepared tins. Cover loosely with clingfilm (plastic wrap) and leave to rise at room temperature for 30–40 minutes, until doubled in size.

4   Preheat the oven to 150°C/300°F/gas mark 2. Score the top of the dough wth a sharp knife, then bake the loaves for 45 minutes. Turn them out, then pop them back inside the tins upside down and bake for a further 10–15 minutes, until the bottom crust is firm. Transfer to a wire rack to cool.

Tips and ideas

Add any of the following at the end of step 2:

*   1 tbsp roasted garlic and 1 tbsp rosemary leaves.

*   75g (½ cup) sultanas (golden raisins) soaked in orange juice.

*   75g (1 cup) roasted red peppers.

*   2 tbsp chopped onion and sage leaves.

*   75g (½ cup) grated mozzarella cheese.

*   50g (2oz) cold cooked bacon pieces.

Multi-seed Guinness Brown Bread

Makes a 900g (2lb) loaf

Sunflower oil, for greasing
50g (⅓ cup) plain (all-purpose) flour
350g (3 cups) wholemeal (whole
 wheat) flour
75g (¾ cup) porridge (rolled) oats
50g (⅓ cup) pinhead oatmeal
 (steel-cut oats)
Pinch of salt
2 tsp bicarbonate of (baking) soda
1 large (US extra large) egg
100ml (½ cup) Guinness
400ml (1⅔ cups) buttermilk
2 tbsp treacle (molasses) (optional)
3 tbsp mixed seeds (e.g. pumpkin,
 sesame, poppy, sunflower)

Packed with flavour, this bread is perfect for serving with soups, stews and cheese. The loaf requires no rising time and should be stirred as little as possible, so it's also really quick to make. It will keep fresh for 4–5 days and is suitable for freezing.

1 Preheat the oven to 160°C/325°F/gas mark 3. Grease a 900g (9 x 5 x 3 inch) loaf tin.

2 Place the flours, oats and salt in a large bowl. Sift in the bicarbonate of soda and stir together. **(a)**

3 Beat the egg in a separate bowl, add to the dry mixture and stir again.

4 Add the Guinness, buttermilk and treacle (if using) and mix to a sloppy consistency. **(b/c)** Finally, stir in 2 tablespoons of the seed mixture. **(d)**

5 Pour into the prepared tin and smooth the top with a wet spoon. **(e/f)** Sprinkle the remaining seeds over the surface and bake for 1 hour. **(g)** Turn the loaf out, then pop it back inside the tin upside down and bake for a further 15–20 minutes. **(h)** Transfer to a wire rack to cool.

Tips and ideas

• When preparing the bread, stir the mixture as little as possible so that it remains light and aerated. For this reason, it is best made by hand rather than machine.

• Sprinkle some extra seeds into the greased baking tin before adding the bread mixture.

a

b

c

d

e

f

g

h

Sticky Malt and Sultana Loaf

Makes a 900g (2lb) loaf

450g (3⅓ cups) strong white flour
(white bread flour), plus extra
for dusting
2 tsp salt
20g (1 small cake) fresh yeast
135ml (½ cup plus 1 tbsp) lukewarm
water
65ml (4 tbsp plus 1 tsp) milk
3 tbsp malt barley extract
2 tbsp sunflower oil, plus extra for
greasing
2 tbsp treacle (molasses)
120g (¾ cup) sultanas (golden raisins)

For the glaze
1 tbsp caster (superfine) sugar
1½ tbsp milk

This sweet bread is scrumptious spread
with butter for a teatime treat.

1　Place the flour and salt in a large bowl.

2　Put the yeast and water in a small bowl and stir until
dissolved. Add the milk, malt extract, oil and treacle.
Pour this liquid into the flour and mix to combine.
Scatter the sultanas over the dough and knead well
for 5–7 minutes.

3　Cover the bowl with clingfilm (plastic wrap) and leave
the dough to rise at room temperature (ideally
24°C/75°F) for 60–75 minutes, until doubled in size.

4　Oil a 900g (9 x 5 x 3 inch) loaf tin and dust with flour.

5　Tip the dough on to a floured work surface and knead
well for 5 minutes. Transfer it to the prepared tin, cover
loosely with oiled clingfilm and leave at room
temperature for about 30 minutes, until the dough
reaches the top of
the tin.

6　Preheat the oven to 200°C/400°F/gas mark 6. Combine
the glaze ingredients in a small bowl.

7　Remove the clingfilm and lightly brush the glaze over
the top of the loaf. Bake for 30–45 minutes, until the
bread is well risen and the underside sounds hollow
when tapped. Transfer to a wire rack to cool.

Tips and ideas

- Add 2 tbsp seeds (e.g. pumpkin, sesame, poppy,
sunflower) for extra crunch.

- This bread goes very well with cheese and chutneys.

Apple Upside-down Cake

Serves 4-6

275g (2½ sticks) butter, plus extra
  for greasing
100g (½ cup) muscovado sugar or
  brown sugar
2-3 Pink Lady apples, peeled, cored
  and each cut into 8 wedges
300g (1½ cups) caster (superfine)
  sugar
3 eggs
350g (2¾ cups) plain (all-purpose)
  flour
2 tsp baking powder
150ml (⅔ cup) milk
1 tsp vanilla extract
Crème anglaise (see page 188) or
  whipped cream, to serve

Although delicious made with apples, this cake can be made with any of your favourite fruits, such as apricots, plums, peaches or pineapple. The muscovado sugar gives a lovely toffee flavour.

1   Grease a 23cm (9 inch) cake tin and line the bottom with nonstick baking (parchment) paper.

2   Melt 75g (6 tbsp) of the butter in a small saucepan. Add the muscovado sugar and leave for 2-3 minutes, until dissolved and starting to combine. Pour the caramel into the prepared tin.

3   Arrange the apple wedges on top of the caramel, then set aside.

4   Preheat the oven to 160°C/325°F/gas mark 3.

5   Put the caster sugar and eggs in a large bowl and whisk until pale and thick enough for the beaters to make a figure of eight on the surface.

6   Sift the flour and baking powder over the egg mixture and gently fold together. Melt the remaining butter and add to the bowl, then pour in the milk and vanilla extract. Mix thoroughly.

7   Pour the batter over the apples and bake for 1-1¼ hours, until the cake is firm to the touch and springs back when lightly pressed.

8   Leave the cake to cool in the tin for 20 minutes, then carefully turn it out, peel off the lining paper and serve warm or cold with crème anglaise or a dollop of cream.

Tips and ideas

- Use caster sugar instead of muscovado sugar for the caramel.

- For extra moistness, add the zest of 1 lemon, or 50ml (¼ cup) apple syrup (we use Highbank Orchard Syrup from Kilkenny).

- When folding the flour into the mixture, try to do so in as few turns as possible to keep the air in it. This will produce a lighter cake.

- It is best to use eating apples rather than cooking apples for this recipe.

Victoria Sponge with Strawberries

Serves 4–6

300g (2½ sticks plus 1 tbsp) butter,
at room temperature, plus extra
for greasing
300g (2⅓ cups) plain (all-purpose)
flour
2 tsp baking powder
300g (1½ cups) caster (superfine)
sugar
5 large (US extra large) eggs
1 tsp vanilla extract

For the filling and topping
6 tbsp strawberry jam
120ml (½ cup) whipped cream
300g (11oz) strawberries, sliced
Icing (confectioners') sugar, for
dusting

Here we have one of my favourite desserts
– great for entertaining. An easy way to
remember the proportions in the recipe is
to weigh the egg and add the same weight
of butter, sugar and flour.

1   Preheat the oven to 180°C/350°F/gas mark 4. Grease
two 20cm (8 inch) cake tins and line the bottoms with
nonstick baking (parchment) paper. **(a)**

2   Place the flour and baking powder in a bowl and
mix together.

3   In a large separate bowl, beat the butter and sugar until
light and fluffy. **(b)** Beat in the eggs and vanilla extract,
then fold in the flour. Divide the batter evenly between
the prepared tins.

4   Bake for 25–30 minutes, or until a skewer or toothpick
inserted in the centre comes out clean. Turn out the
sponges on to a wire rack and leave to cool.

5   To sandwich the cake together, peel off the lining papers
and spread half the jam on each sponge. Cover the jam
on one sponge with the whipped cream and sliced
strawberries. Place the second sponge on top, jam-side
down. Dust with icing sugar.

a

b

Tips and ideas

- Use berry compote (see page 208) instead of jam.

- Try other fillings, such as mascarpone, crème fraîche
mixed with strawberry purée or lemon curd.

- The filling can be piped on top of your cake if you want
to make it even more decorative. Half-fill a piping (pastry)
bag fitted with a 1cm (½ inch) star nozzle (tip) and twist
closed to make sure it contains no air pockets. You can start
by practising on a piece of nonstick baking (parchment)
paper if you like. Remember that mistakes can be scraped
off and you can start again.

Sticky Toffee Puddings

Makes 12–16 individual puddings

200g (1¾ sticks) butter, at room
   temperature, plus extra for greasing
300g (2 cups) stoned (pitted) dates
300ml (1¼ cups) water
10g (2 tsp) bicarbonate of (baking)
   soda
400g (2 cups) caster (superfine) sugar
4 eggs
350g (2¾ cups) plain (all-purpose)
   flour
20g (2 tsp) baking powder
30ml (2 tbsp) milk
1 tsp vanilla extract
1 tsp five-spice powder

For the toffee sauce
225g (2 sticks) salted butter
225g (1 cup) brown sugar
300ml (1¼ cups) double (heavy)
   cream

A cross between a dessert and a cake, this is both sweet and moist, a firm family favourite. Toffee sauce is basically butterscotch sauce that is cooked for longer to make it darker and more intense. If you'd prefer it lighter, cook the caramel until it is pale and golden in colour.

1   Preheat the oven to 160°C/325°F/gas mark 3. Grease 12–16 small cake tins or ramekins (the number depends on their capacity).

2   Place the dates and water in a large saucepan and bring to the boil. Add the bicarbonate of soda and simmer for 3–5 minutes. **(a)** Leave to cool for 10 minutes. Using a food processor or hand blender, blend the mixture to a coarse sticky consistency, then set aside. **(b)**

3   Put the butter and caster sugar into a bowl and beat until light and fluffy. Add the eggs, sift in the flour and baking powder, then continue beating until smooth. **(c)** Pour in the milk, then add the vanilla, spice and cooled date mixture. Mix well. **(d)**

4   Half-fill the prepared cake tins with the batter and bake for 20 minutes, or until a skewer or toothpick inserted in the centre comes out clean. **(e)**

5   Meanwhile, make the toffee sauce. Put the butter, brown sugar and cream into a large saucepan over a medium-low heat and bring to the boil. **(f/g)** Reduce the heat and cook without stirring for 3–5 minutes, until the mixture is dark and intensely flavoured. **(h)** Be careful not to burn the caramel or yourself.

6   Leave the cakes to cool in the tins for 5 minutes, then turn them out on to serving plates. Pour the toffee sauce over them and serve at once.

Tips and ideas

- Serve the pudding with ice cream sprinkled with chopped walnuts to add extra texture.

e

f

g

h

Very Berry Jelly Terrine

Serves 4-6

4-6 gelatine leaves or sheets
350ml (1½ cups) clear apple juice
75g (⅓ cup) caster (superfine) sugar
1-2 drops of red food colouring
250g (2 cups) raspberries
200g (1½ cups) blueberries
200g (1¼ cups) strawberries,
   halved

For a speedy dessert, you can simply combine all the fruit in the mould and pour the jelly (gelatin) over the top. For something that looks far more impressive, layer the fruits as suggested below.

1   Put the gelatine leaves in a small bowl, cover with cold water and leave to soak for 5 minutes. **(a)**

2   Pour half the apple juice into a small saucepan and add the sugar. Place over a low heat until the sugar has dissolved. Remove from the heat and stir in the squeezed-out gelatine. **(b)**

3   Put the remaining apple juice in a large jug (pitcher) or bowl and pour in the gelatine mixture. Add the colouring and stir once to combine.

4   Arrange the raspberries in a single layer in the bottom of a 500ml (1 pint) jelly mould. This will be the top layer when turned out, so make sure it looks good!

5   Pour in just enough of the gelatine syrup to come halfway up the raspberries, then place in the refrigerator for 10-15 minutes, or until set.

6   Make another two layers with the remaining fruit and jelly in the same way, allowing each layer to set before adding the next one. Finally, place the terrine in the refrigerator overnight, or for at least 4 hours.

7   To unmould the jelly, place the dish in warm water for 10-15 seconds, then invert on to a serving plate. Cut the jelly into slices at the table and serve with lightly whipped cream or ice cream.

a

b

Tips and ideas

- Gelatine is derived from animal collagen, and is sold in powder and leaf form. The powder needs to be dissolved in cold water until it swells, and is then added to warm liquid. Leaf gelatine must be immersed in cold water for about 5 minutes until it becomes pliable; it is then squeezed dry and added to warm liquid.

Vanilla Bavarois with Poached Rhubarb

Serves 6

10 gelatine leaves or sheets
400ml (1⅔ cups) milk
3 vanilla pods or beans, slit open
   lengthways
6 egg yolks
100g (½ cup) caster (superfine) sugar
400ml (1⅔ cups) double (heavy)
   cream

For the poached rhubarb
400g (2 cups) caster sugar
1 vanilla pod or bean, slit open
   lengthways
2 cardamom pods
1 star anise
900ml (3¾ cups) water
100ml (½ cup) white wine
Zest and juice of ½ lemon
400g (14oz) rhubarb (about 8 stalks),
   chopped into 2.5cm (1 inch) pieces

Tips and ideas

- Use any fruit you like to flavour the crème anglaise. Raspberry purée is particularly delicious.

- Note that certain fruits, such as kiwi, papaya, pineapple, oranges and figs, contain an enzyme that prevents gelatine from setting, particularly if they are used in large quantities. To avoid this, cook the fruit first, or use canned fruit; both processes destroy the enzyme.

Bavarois or Bavarian cream is a set custard or crème anglaise flavoured and lightened with whipped cream. It's sinfully delicious.

1   Put the gelatine in a small bowl, cover with cold water and leave to soak for 5 minutes.

2   Pour the milk into a saucepan. Scrape in the vanilla seeds and add the pods, then heat slowly until simmering. Leave to infuse for 5 minutes. **(a)**

3   Put the egg yolks and sugar in a large bowl and whisk until pale and fluffy. **(b)** Pour in half the milk mixture, stirring gently with a wooden spoon. Return it to the saucepan and place over a low heat, stirring constantly until thick enough to coat the back of the spoon. Remove from the heat immediately.

4   Squeeze the gelatine dry, then stir it into the egg mixture. **(c)** Strain through a fine sieve or strainer into a large bowl set over ice. **(d)** Stir constantly for 4–5 minutes, until the crème anglaise has cooled but not yet set.

5   Put the cream into a bowl, then whip gently to soft peaks.

6   Fold the cream into the crème anglaise, then pour into six individual glass dishes and chill for 2–3 hours, until set. **(e/f)**

7   Meanwhile, prepare a poaching syrup for the rhubarb. Place the sugar, vanilla pod, cardamom, star anise, water, wine, lemon zest and juice in a saucepan, bring to the boil, then reduce the heat and simmer for 3–4 minutes. **(g)** Remove from the heat and strain through a fine sieve or strainer into a glass bowl, discarding the solids.

8   Pour the syrup into a saucepan and bring to a gentle simmer. Add the rhubarb and poach gently for 2 minutes, then set aside for 2–4 minutes. The rhubarb should be tender but still holding its shape. Using a slotted spoon, carefully lift the rhubarb out of the syrup and transfer to a plate to cool. **(h)** Save the syrup for using in sorbets, smoothies or cocktails.

9   Serve the bavarois with the poached rhubarb placed on top.

a

b

c

d

Chocolate

Cooking with Chocolate

Chocolate comes from the *Theobroma cacao* tree, which is believed to have originated in the Amazon rainforest in South America. The beans are the source of chocolate, which Aztecs regarded as the 'food of the gods', and they were also used as a currency for bartering goods. Around 1502 the explorer Christopher Columbus became the first person to introduce cocoa beans to Europe. Many people viewed them with suspicion, and it took another 40 years for chocolate to catch on, by which time the explorer Hernán Cortez was credited with its introduction.

Like peas, cocoa beans grow in pods, but in this case on trees about 12–18m (40–60ft) tall. The trees have wide branches and now grow wild in several other areas of the world, including Central America, Africa and tropical parts of Asia.

The taste of the chocolate has a lot to do with how it's made, not least the proportion of cocoa solids and the amount of additives it contains. Cheap milk chocolate can have a very sweet taste and waxy texture, while low-quality dark chocolate can taste harsh. Many small, independent chocolatiers aim for a more refined taste in their products.

Dark chocolate: Pure, unsweetened chocolate contains 100 per cent cocoa solids, no other ingredients or additives and has a very bitter flavour. The dark (semisweet) chocolate we buy in shops has been mixed with sugar and cocoa butter (the fatty part of the bean) to make it more palatable, and contains anywhere from 35 to 80 per cent cocoa solids. The higher the percentage, the more expensive the chocolate. Similarly, the greater the health benefits, because dark chocolate contains significant amounts of antioxidants, fibre, iron, magnesium, copper and manganese. However, it's important to remember that chocolate also contains significant amounts of fat and sugar.

Milk chocolate: The proportion of cocoa solids in milk chocolate ranges from 20 to 30 per cent, and the fat and sugar content tend to be much higher than in dark chocolate. The solids are 'diluted' with milk, sugar and cream, giving the chocolate a smoother, creamier taste with virtually no hint of bitterness. Most mass-market chocolate bars are made from milk chocolate.

White chocolate: It has been argued that white chocolate isn't chocolate at all because it contains no cocoa solids. It is actually a confection made from cocoa butter, sugar, milk, lecithin and vanilla. Nonetheless, it is a very popular product and has many uses in cooking, particularly for decorating cakes and desserts. It makes a wonderful contrast to dark chocolate.

How to temper chocolate

The process of tempering chocolate is necessary to make it more malleable for dipping and coating, and to ensure it stays shiny and snappy once it has set. One of the best ways of doing this is a process called 'seeding', which involves melting two-thirds of the required amount of chocolate in a bain-marie, or water bath, and then adding the remaining third to it. This encourages the cocoa butter crystals to return to their original state once they set.

If, for some reason, the tempered chocolate doesn't come out right, you can always repeat the process, meaning that no chocolate is wasted.

Temper about 300g (11oz) of chocolate at a time. It's hard to temper smaller amounts because it's difficult to keep the temperature stable.

Milk and white chocolate are tempered in the same way as dark (semisweet) chocolate, but the temperatures differ slightly (see steps 3, 6 and 7).

1   Chop the chocolate evenly and finely. **(a)**

2   Place about 200g (7oz) of chocolate in a heatproof bowl set over a saucepan of simmering water, making sure the bottom of the bowl does not touch the water. **(b)**

3   Place a sugar (candy) thermometer in the bowl and melt the chocolate, stirring with a rubber spatula to make sure is melts evenly. Keep an eye on the thermometer to ensure the temperature does not exceed the following:

Dark chocolate: 55–58°C/130–136°F

Milk chocolate: 44–50°C/113–122°F

White chocolate: 44–50°C/113–122°F

4   When the chocolate has melted, remove the bowl from heat and wipe the bottom to remove condensation. **(c)** You want to avoid any chance of getting water in the chocolate or it could seize up into a chunky mess.

5   Stir the remaining 100g (4oz) of chocolate into the melted chocolate and leave that to melt too. **(d)**

6   The chocolate will start cooling and thickening as you add the unmelted chocolate. The temperature it must drop to is as follows:

Dark chocolate: 28–29°C/82–84°F

Milk chocolate: 28°C/82°F

White chocolate: 26°C/79°F

When the chocolate has dropped to the right temperature, set the bowl back over the pan of simmering water over a low heat. **(e)**

7   Heat the chocolate back to the following temperatures:

Dark chocolate: 31–33°C/88–91°F

Milk chocolate: 30°C/86°F

White chocolate: 28–29°C/82–84°F

Be sure to stir and watch carefully so that the chocolate warms evenly. If any bit of it exceeds the maximum temperature, the chocolate will be out of temper and you'll have to start all over again.

8   To test for readiness, spread a little of the tempered chocolate on a piece of nonstick baking (parchment) paper or greaseproof (wax) paper. **(f)** If it dries shiny with no streaks, it's good to go!

Chocolate Fondants

Serves 4

200g (7oz) dark (semisweet)
  chocolate (at least 70 per cent
  cocoa solids), broken into pieces
100g (1 stick) butter, cubed
3 eggs, separated
100g (½ cup) caster (superfine) sugar
Pouring (light) cream, to serve

These chocolate fondants are very rich and indulgent. Good-quality chocolate makes all the difference, so try to get some with a high percentage of cocoa solids.

1 Preheat the oven to 180°C/350°F/gas mark 4.

2 Melt the chocolate in a heatproof bowl set over a saucepan of simmering water, making sure the bottom of the bowl does not touch the water. **(a)** Remove the bowl from the heat and stir in the butter until melted. **(b)** Leave to cool for 2–3 minutes.

3 Put the egg yolks and half the sugar into a separate bowl and beat until pale and fluffy. Add the chocolate mixture and beat again.

4 Place the egg whites in a third spotlessly clean bowl and whisk until they form stiff peaks. Gradually whisk in the remaining sugar a little at a time, until you have a stiff and shiny meringue.

5 Fold the meringue into the chocolate mixture, then spoon into four ovenproof porcelain teacups or ramekins, filling them two-thirds full. Arrange on a baking sheet and bake for 12 minutes, until well risen but still with a slight wobble in the middle.

6 Serve hot, with the cream on the side.

a

b

Tips and ideas

• If you want to present your fondant in one large dish, add 25g (3 tbsp) plain (all-purpose) flour to the chocolate mixture before folding in the meringue. This will help it to stand firm.

• To improve the appearance of the fondant, lightly coat the mould with some cocoa powder. This prevents sticking and makes it look more attractive.

Chocolate and Pistachio Fudge

Makes 12–16 squares

50g (4 tbsp) butter, cubed, plus extra
  for greasing
400g (2 cups) caster (superfine) sugar
40g (½ cup) unsweetened cocoa
  powder
½ tsp salt
225ml (1 cup) milk
2 tsp vanilla extract
100g (¾ cup) pistachio nuts, crushed

Tips and ideas

- Butter the sides of saucepan before starting to cook, and don't stir or knock the pan when it's cooling. These steps should ensure that your fudge will be creamier and almost never crystallize.

- If you're lucky enough to have an Aga, you will be able to maintain a constant very low heat much more easily and thus reduce the risk of the mixture crystallizing or burning.

- It might take 20 minutes or more for the sugar to reach the soft ball stage, so be patient!

- When the fudge is nearing the soft ball stage, the bubbles will become smaller and tighter. Begin testing as soon as you notice this change.

- To make this fudge suitable for those who are lactose intolerant, use coconut milk and coconut oil instead of the dairy products. You can also omit the nuts if you like.

Home-made fudge is a delight, but sometimes tricky to get right. If yours overcooks and crystallizes, all is not lost. Simply add it to mugs of hot chocolate for a delicious treat.

1   Grease a small, shallow baking pan and line it with nonstick baking (parchment) paper, allowing the paper to slightly overhang the edges. Fill a bowl with water and ice cubes.

2   Put the sugar, cocoa powder and salt in a heavy-based saucepan, add the milk and whisk until combined. **(a)**

3   Place the pan over a low-medium heat and bring the mixture to a light boil, stirring occasionally with a spatula to ensure it doesn't stick to the bottom. **(b)** Keep the heat as low as possible and don't stir too often or the fudge will become grainy. Skim off any scum that rises to the surface.

4   After about 10–15 minutes, the mixture is ready when it reaches 117°C/235°F or the soft ball stage. **(c)** (To test for this, drizzle a little of it into the iced water. If it forms a soft, pliable ball, it's done.) **(d)**

5   Remove immediately from the heat and place the pan in the cold water, being very careful not to get any splashes in it. **(e)** Leave to stand until the temperature drops to about 50°C/115°F.

6   Add the vanilla extract, pistachios and butter and beat with a wooden spoon until fairly cool but still liquid. **(f/g)**

7   Transfer the fudge to the prepared pan. It should be liquid enough to spread out evenly on its own. **(h)** Leave to set overnight at room temperature, or in the refrigerator for 4–6 hours, before cutting it.

a

b

c

d

e

f

g

h

Chocolate-iced Yogurt Cupcakes

Makes about 12

3 eggs
200g (1 cup) caster (superfine) sugar
120ml (½ cup) natural (plain) yogurt
120g (1 stick) butter, melted
300g (2⅓ cups) plain (all-purpose)
   flour
100g (¾ cup) cornflour (cornstarch)
2 tsp baking powder
Zest of ½ orange
2 tsp vanilla extract
100g (4oz) dark (semisweet)
   chocolate, at least 70 per cent cocoa
   solids, chopped into small pieces
Icing (confectioners') sugar, for
   dusting

For the icing

165g (5½oz) white chocolate, chopped
   into small pieces
375ml (1⅔ cups) double (heavy) cream
Zest of ½ orange or 1 tsp vanilla
   extract

Tips and ideas

- Add berries or other fruits, tossing them in flour before adding them to the cupcake mixture.

- To make dark chocolate icing, use 90g (3½oz) dark (semisweet) chocolate (at least 70 per cent cocoa solids) and 300ml (1⅓ cups) double (heavy) cream – 100ml (⅓ cup) of it hot, and 200ml (1 cup) of it cold, as in step 2.

- To make buttercream icing, beat 200g (1¾ sticks) butter with 400g (3¼ cups) icing (confectioners') sugar until light and fluffy. Place in a piping (pastry) bag fitted with a star-shaped nozzle (tip) and swirl in 4 tbsp ready-made chocolate sauce. Pipe over the cupcakes as above.

These cupcakes are beautifully moist and very addictive. Icing them takes a bit of time, but the finished result looks fantastic.

1   First make the icing. Melt the chocolate in a heatproof bowl set over a small saucepan of simmering water, making sure the bottom of the bowl does not touch the water. **(a)**

2   Put 120ml (½ cup) of the cream in a second small saucepan and bring to the boil. Remove from the heat and pour the cream into the melted chocolate one-third at a time, stirring briskly after each addition to create a shiny mixture. **(b)**

3   Pour the remaining cold cream into the chocolate, add your chosen flavouring and stir thoroughly. **(c/d)** Cover with clingfilm (plastic wrap) and place in the refrigerator for 3 hours.

4   Preheat the oven to 180°C/350°F/gas mark 4. Line a 12-hole muffin tin with paper cases (liners).

5   Put the eggs and caster sugar into a large bowl and whisk together until light and fluffy, or until a figure of eight holds its shape on the mixture for a few seconds.

6   Add the yogurt, then the melted butter. Gently fold in the flour, cornflour and baking powder, then add the orange zest, vanilla extract and chocolate pieces.

7   Divide the batter between the paper cases, then dust the top of each with a little icing sugar. Bake for 12–15 minutes, or until cooked through. **(e)** Transfer to a wire rack to cool.

8   Lightly whisk the chilled icing until smooth and light. **(f)** Place in a piping (pastry) bag fitted with a star-shaped nozzle (tip) and pipe in spirals on top of the cupcakes. **(g/h)**

e

f

g

h

Milk Chocolate Marquise

Serves 8–10

275ml (1 cup plus 2 tbsp) double (heavy) cream
40g (⅓ cup) icing (confectioners') sugar
4 egg yolks
100g (½ cup) caster (superfine) sugar
200g (1¾ sticks) butter
75g (1 cup) unsweetened cocoa powder
75g (3oz) milk chocolate, melted
100g (½ cup) canned Amarena cherries, drained and stoned (pitted)

A marquise is a delicate dessert, somewhere between a mousse and a parfait. It can be made with any type of chocolate and I defy anyone not to love it! Serve with a berry compote (see tips below) and whipped cream.

1   Line a 900g (9 x 5 x 3 inch) loaf tin with a double layer of clingfilm (plastic wrap), allowing it to overhang the edges.

2   Put the cream and icing sugar into a bowl, whip gently to soft peaks, then place in the refrigerator until required.

3   Put the egg yolks and caster sugar into another bowl and whisk until the mixture has more than doubled in volume and holds a figure of eight shape on the surface. **(a)**

4   Place the butter and cocoa powder in a heatproof bowl set over a saucepan of simmering water, making sure the bottom of the bowl does not touch the water, and allow the butter to melt. Fold into the yolk mixture, then gently fold in the melted chocolate. The mixture will thicken slightly.

5   Gently incorporate the reserved whipped cream, then stir in the cherries. **(b)**

6   Transfer the mixture to the prepared loaf tin, fold the clingfilm over the top and leave to set in the freezer for up to 12 hours.

a

b

Tips and ideas

•   To give your marquise a crunchy base like a cheesecake, sprinkle it with chopped nuts and/or crushed biscuits (cookies) before turning it out on to a serving platter.

•   To make a simple berry compote, place about 225g (2 cups) summer berries such as raspberries and blackberries into a saucepan with 25g (2 tbsp) caster (superfine) sugar and 25ml (2 tbsp) Grand Marnier, and simmer for 3–4 minutes. Serve warm or cold.

Profiteroles with Chocolate Sauce

Serves 4-6

2 quantities Choux Pastry (see page 50)
1 egg yolk mixed with 1 tsp milk, for brushing
250ml (1 cup) whipped cream or crème patissière (see page 52)

For the chocolate sauce
150g (5oz) dark (semisweet) chocolate (at least 70 per cent cocoa solids), broken into pieces
250ml (1 cup) double (heavy) cream
25g (2 tbsp) softened butter

Profiteroles are small choux buns that can be made in a variety of sizes and filled with a custard-like crème patissière or whipped cream.

1 Preheat the oven to 160°C/325°F/gas mark 3. Line a baking sheet with nonstick baking (parchment) paper.

2 Spoon the dough into a piping (pastry) bag fitted with a plain 1cm (½ inch) nozzle (tip). Pipe walnut-sized mounds on to the prepared baking sheet, spacing them at least 2.5cm (1 inch) apart.

3 Dip a fork into a bowl of hot water and smooth the top of each mound. Brush the top of each mound with a very light coating of egg wash.

4 Bake for 30-35 minutes, until golden brown outside and dry inside. Transfer to a wire rack to cool.

5 Meanwhile, prepare the chocolate sauce. Place the chocolate in a heatproof bowl. Bring the cream to the boil in a small saucepan, then pour half of it over the chocolate. Stir to combine, then add the remaining cream (this will prevent the mixture splitting). Add the butter and stir until smooth. Cover with clingfilm (plastic wrap) and keep warm until required.

6 Before serving, spoon your chosen filling into a piping bag fitted with a 5mm (¼ inch) nozzle. Use a sharp knife, skewer or toothpick to make a small hole in the bottom of each bun, then insert the nozzle and fill. **(a/b)**

7 Place the filled buns on a serving platter and drizzle the chocolate sauce over them.

Tips and ideas

- Before piping the buns on to the parchment-lined baking sheet, sprinkle it with a few drop of water. This will help to create steam in the oven and give the buns a better rise.

- Add the seeds from a vanilla pod or bean to the cream before whipping it.

- For a lighter chocolate sauce replace 100ml (½ cup) of the cream with water.

Opéra-style Chocolate Cake

Serves 12–16

90g (3½oz) dark (semisweet)
  chocolate (at least 70 per cent
  cocoa solids)
135g (1 stick plus 1½ tbsp) butter,
  softened
135g (⅔ cup) caster (superfine) sugar
2 eggs
65g (½ cup) plain (all-purpose) flour

For the dark chocolate mousse
125g (4½oz) dark chocolate
  (at least 70 per cent cocoa solids),
  chopped
1 egg, separated
250ml (1 cup) double (heavy) cream,
  lightly whipped to soft peaks

For the milk chocolate mousse
125g (4½oz) milk chocolate
  (33 per cent cocoa solids), chopped
1 egg, separated
200ml (¾ cup plus 2 tbsp) double
  cream, lightly whipped

For the white chocolate mousse
125g (4½oz) white chocolate (28 per
  cent cocoa solids), chopped
1 egg, separated
200ml (¾ cup plus 2 tbsp) double
  cream, lightly whipped

For the chocolate glaze
90g (3½oz) dark chocolate
  (at least 70 per cent cocoa solids),
  finely chopped
150ml (⅔ cup) double cream
30ml (2 tbsp) water
40g (3 tbsp) runny honey
25g (2 tbsp) butter, cubed

The classic Opéra gateau is a multi-layered sponge cake sandwiched together with chocolate ganache and buttercream and topped with fruit. Here is my take on it, which uses brownie-style chocolate sponge, three types of chocolate mousse and chocolate glazing. It should be prepared a day before required, because it's quite complicated and must be frozen overnight.

1   Preheat the oven to 180°C/350°F/gas mark 4. Line three 22 x 22cm (9 x 9 inch) baking sheets with greaseproof (wax) paper.

Sponge

2   Melt the chocolate in a heatproof bowl set over a saucepan of simmering water, making sure the bottom of the bowl does not touch the water.

3   Put the butter in another bowl and beat until soft.

4   Place the sugar and eggs in a third bowl and beat until pale and fluffy.

5   Remove the chocolate from the heat and fold in the soft butter. Combine with the egg mixture, then sift in the flour. Mix with spatula until no pockets of flour are left.

6   Divide the mixture equally among the prepared baking sheets and spread into an even layer 5mm (¼ inch) thick. **(a)** Bake for 6–8 minutes. Transfer to a wire rack to cool.

Dark chocolate mousse

7   Melt the chocolate in a heatproof bowl set over a saucepan of simmering water, making sure the bottom of the bowl does not touch the water. Leave to cool slightly, until about 45–50°C/113–122°F.

8   Lightly beat the egg yolk, then add to the melted chocolate and stir well with a spatula. **(b)** Fold in one-third of the whipped cream, then whisk in the remainder. **(c)** It will soften the mixture and loosen its consistency.

9   Put the egg white into a clean bowl and whisk until stiff. Gently fold into the chocolate cream mixture. **(d)** Set aside.

Milk chocolate mousse

10 Make in the same way as the dark chocolate mousse.

White chocolate mousse

11 Make in the same way as the dark chocolate mousse.

To build the cake

12 Line a deep baking tin 22 x 22cm (9 x 9 inches) with three layers of clingfilm (plastic wrap), allowing it to generously overhang the edges. Build the layers of the cake as follows: sponge, dark chocolate mousse, sponge, milk chocolate mousse, sponge, white chocolate mousse. **(e/f)** Cover with the overhanging clingfilm and freeze overnight.

Chocolate glaze

13 Melt the chocolate in a heatproof bowl set over a saucepan of simmering water, making sure the bottom of the bowl does not touch the water.

14 Put the cream, water and honey in a small saucepan and bring to the boil.

15 Pour one-third of the boiled cream mixture on to the melted chocolate and mix with a spatula until shiny. Add another third, combine again, then add the final third. Leave to cool to 35–40°C/95–104°F, then add the butter.

16 Place the frozen cake on a wire rack over a tray (to catch any drips) and pour the glaze over it. **(g)** Spread it out smoothly with a rubber spatula or palette knife, then place in the refrigerator for 4–6 hours to set.

17 Before serving, trim the cake edges evenly using a knife dipped in warm water. **(h)** Use the same technique to cut the cake into slices.

Mendiants

Makes about 40

300g (11oz) dark (semisweet)
  chocolate (at least 70 per cent
  cocoa solids)
200g (generous 1 cup) mixture of
  dried fruits, nuts, crystallized ginger
  and candied peel

A mendiant is a little chocolate disc that is
usually topped with nuts, fruit or candied
peel. Children love making them, and can
use whatever colourful toppings they like.

1 Place two or three sheets of nonstick baking
   (parchment) paper on a flat, cold surface in a cool area.

2 Temper the chocolate as described on page 196.

3 Using a tablespoon, drop 1 small spoonful of chocolate
   at a time on to the paper and use the back of the spoon
   to flatten it into an even circle about 4cm (1½ inches)
   wide and 3mm (⅛ inch) thick. **(a)** When you have made
   6–10 circles, decorate them with the mixed fruits and
   nuts. **(b)** It's important to work in batches so that the
   decoration is added before the chocolate has set.

4 When each batch is complete, set the sheet aside until
   the chocolate hardens. Using a palette knife (spatula),
   carefully lift the mendiants off the sheets. They can be
   eaten straight away, or will keep for 2–3 weeks in an
   airtight container (not in the refrigerator).

a

b

Index

Page numbers in *italic* refer to the illustrations

Acknowledgements

Again, I would like to thank the fantastic team at Octopus Publishing Group, particularly Denise Bates for believing in the book and commissioning it; Clare Churly for capturing the style and vision I had for this book; Juliette Norsworthy for her exceptional design and attention to detail; Kate Blinman, home economist; Brid Ni Luasaigh, photographer's assistant; and Caroline Alberti for managing the production of this book. My sincerest gratitude to Cristian Barnett for the creative photography, an absolute pleasure to work with.

A massive thank you to my team of Julien Clémot, Development Chef, and Niamh Donegan, Personal Assistant, for their unwavering support and dedication. I'd also like to thank my team at Dunbrody House for their enthusiasm for all our tastings and their continuous support.

None of this would have been possible without the hard work of my agent Martine Carter and my US Manager Brandon Evans.

Finally, thanks to the team at Ted Baker, Dublin for supplying my wardrobe for the photography.

Group Publishing Director: Denise Bates

Project Editor: Clare Churly

Senior Art Editor: Juliette Norsworthy

Home Economist: Kate Blinman

Stylist: Jessica Georgiades

Photographer: Cristian Barnett

Assistant Production Manager: Caroline Alberti